Naked and Fiery Forms

Naked and Fiery Forms

Modern American Poetry by Women, A New Tradition

SUZANNE JUHASZ

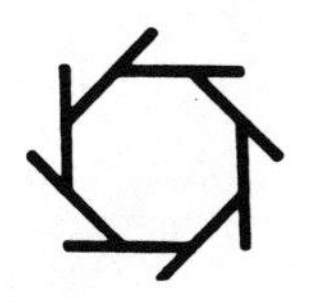

OCTAGON BOOKS

A DIVISION OF FARRAR, STRAUS AND GIROUX

New York 1978

Published 1976

Second Octagon printing 1978

OCTAGON BOOKS
A DIVISION OF FARRAR, STRAUS & GIROUX, INC.
19 Union Square West
New York, N.Y. 10003

Library of Congress Cataloging in Publication Data

Juhasz, Suzanne, 1942-
Naked and fiery forms.

Bibliography: p.
1. Women poets, American—20th century.
PS151.J8 1976 811'.5'09 76-16672
ISBN 0-374-94450-4

Manufactured by Braun-Brumfield, Inc.
Ann Arbor, Michigan
Printed in the United States of America

Contents

Acknowledgments

I thank my students of poetry by women at the University of Colorado and at San José State University, as well as my colleagues and friends across the country; their responses and suggestions have encouraged, challenged, and supported me in the writing of this book. Special thanks to Aladeen Smith, whose skill in editing and typing the manuscript was a major contribution.

The title quotation is from Adrienne Rich's poem, "Blood-Sister." Portions of this book have appeared in *Frontiers: A Journal of Women Studies* and in *San José Studies*.

I wish to thank the following publishers for their permission to quote from published works:

Aphra, for permission to quote, "Emily Dickinson Postage Stamp" by Lynn Strongin, which first appeared in *Aphra* 3:3 (Summer 1972).

The Bobbs-Merrill Company, Inc., for permission to quote from Nikki Giovanni, *Gemini*, 1971.

Broadside Press for permission to quote from Nikki Giovanni, *Re: Creation*, 1970. Also for permission to quote from Gwendolyn Brooks, *Family Pictures*, copyright © 1973 by Gwendolyn Brooks.

Chatto and Windus, Ltd., for permission to quote from Adrienne Rich, *Necessities of Life*, 1966; *Snapshots of a Daughter-in-Law*, 1967; *Leaflets*, 1969; and *The Will to Change*, 1971.

The Crossing Press, for permission to quote from Alta, *I Am Not a Practicing Angel*, 1975.

Faber and Faber, Ltd., for permission to quote from *The Complete Poems of Marianne Moore*, 1967. Reprinted by permission of Faber and Faber, Ltd.

Harper and Row Publishers, Inc., for permission to quote from Sylvia Plath, *Ariel*, copyright © 1965 by Ted Hughes; *Crossing the Water*, copyright © 1971 by Ted Hughes; *Winter Trees*, copyright © 1972 by Ted Hughes. Reprinted by permission of Harper and Row Publishers, Inc. Also for permission to quote from *The World of Gwendolyn Brooks*, 1971, copyright © 1945, 1949, 1960, 1968 by Gwendolyn Brooks Blakely, and from Gwendolyn Brooks, *Selected Poems*, copyright © 1963 by Gwendolyn Brooks Blakely. Reprinted by permission of Harper and Row Publishers, Inc.

Harvard University Press, for permission to quote from *The Poems of Emily Dickinson*. Reprinted by permission of the publishers and the Trustees of Amherst College from *The Poems of Emily Dickinson*, edited by Thomas H. Johnson, Cambridge, Massachusetts: The Belknap Press of Harvard University Press. Copyright © 1951, 1955 by the President and Fellows of Harvard College.

Gerald Hausman, for permission to quote "Sleeping Out."

Houghton Mifflin, Co., for permission to quote from *The Complete Poetical Works of Amy Lowell*, 1955. Also for permission to quote from Anne Sexton, *To Bedlam and Part Way Back*, 1960; *Live or Die*, 1966; *Transformations*, 1971; *The Book of Folly*, 1973; and *The Death Notebooks*, 1974.

Olwyn Hughes, for permission to quote from Sylvia Plath, *The Colossus*, Faber and Faber, London, copyright © 1960 by Sylvia Plath and 1967 by Ted Hughes; from *Ariel*, Faber and Faber, London, copyright © 1965 by Ted Hughes; from *Crossing the Water* and *Winter Trees*, Faber and Faber, London, copyright © 1971 by Ted Hughes.

Nancy Esther James, for permission to quote "The Poems of Women," by Suzanne Juhasz, which appeared in *I, That Am Ever Stranger: Poems on Women's Experience*, ed. Nancy E. James (New Wilmington, Pa.: Globe Printing Company, 1974).

Alfred A. Knopf, Inc., for permission to quote from Sylvia Plath, *The Colossus and Other Poems*, 1968.

Little, Brown and Co., for permission to quote from *The Complete Poems of Emily Dickinson*, edited by Thomas H. Johnson, 1955: #306, #1695 copyright 1914, 1942 by Martha Dickinson Bianchi; #657, #695, copyright 1929, © 1957 by Mary L. Hampson; #613,

#383, #405, copyright 1935 by Martha Dickinson Bianchi, copyright © renewed 1963 by Mary L. Hampson.

The Sterling Lord Agency, Inc., for permission to quote from Anne Sexton, *Live or Die,* 1966; *Transformations,* 1971; *The Book of Folly,* 1973; and *The Death Notebooks,* 1974.

Macmillan Publishing Co., Inc., for permission to quote from *The Collected Poems of Marianne Moore.* Reprinted with permission of Macmillan Publishing Co., Inc., from *Collected Poems* by Marianne Moore, copyright 1951 by Marianne Moore; copyright 1935 by Marianne Moore, renewed 1963 by Marianne Moore and T. S. Eliot; copyright 1944 by Marianne Moore, renewed 1972 by Marianne Moore.

William Morrow and Company, Inc., for permission to quote from Nikki Giovanni, *Black Feeling, Black Talk/Black Judgement,* copyright © 1968, 1970 by Nikki Giovanni, and Nikki Giovanni, *My House,* copyright © 1972 by Nikki Giovanni. Reprinted by permission of William Morrow and Company, Inc.

New Directions Publishing Corporation, for permission to quote from Denise Levertov, *O Taste and See,* copyright © 1964 by Denise Levertov Goodman, reprinted by permission of New Directions Publishing Corporation; *The Sorrow Dance,* copyright © 1955 © 1966 by Denise Levertov Goodman ("Life at War" and "Olga Poems" were first published in *Poetry*), reprinted by permission of New Directions Publishing Corporation; *Footprints,* copyright © 1970, 1971, 1972 by Denise Levertov Goodman, reprinted by permission of New Directions Publishing Corporation; *To Stay Alive,* copyright © 1971 by Denise Levertov Goodman, reprinted by permission of New Directions Publishing Corporation; *Relearning the Alphabet,* copyright © 1969, 1970 by Denise Levertov Goodman, reprinted by permission of New Directions Publishing Corporation. Also for permission to quote from William Carlos Williams, *Collected Earlier Poems,* copyright 1938 by New Directions Publishing Corporation. Reprinted by permission of New Directions Publishing Corporation.

W. W. Norton and Company, Inc., for permission to quote from Adrienne Rich, *Necessities of Life,* 1966; *Snapshots of a Daughter-in-Law,* 1967; *Leaflets,* 1969; *The Will to Change,* 1971; *Diving into the Wreck,* 1973; and *Poems: Selected and New,* 1975.

Oxford University Press, for permission to quote from M. L. Rosenthal, *The New Poets.*

Laurence Pollinger, Ltd., for permission to quote from Denise Levertov, *The Sorrow Dance, The Jacob's Ladder,* and *Relearning the Alphabet,* Jonathan Cape Ltd., publishers.

Shameless Hussy Press, for permission to quote from Alta, *No Visible Means of Support,* 1971, and *Letters to Women.*

The Viking Press, for permission to quote from *The Complete Poems of Marianne Moore,* copyright © 1959 by Marianne Moore. All rights reserved. Reprinted by permission of The Viking Press, Inc.

1

The Double Bind of the Woman Poet

Until the twentieth century, there was no body of poetry by women in English. Now one exists: I should like to characterize it as a new tradition, one that speaks in the voice of women, rather than in a pseudo-male or neuter voice. The old tradition has been masculine: an expression and reflection of the male norms and values of a patriarchal culture. This book traces the development of the new tradition by examining closely the work of some of the poets who have created it: Emily Dickinson, Marianne Moore, Denise Levertov, Sylvia Plath, Anne Sexton, Gwendolyn Brooks, Nikki Giovanni, Alta, and Adrienne Rich.

Being a woman poet is a peculiar social and psychological situation, to which the poetry that women write is related. For the poem does not spring fully formed from a father's head: it is created by a woman who is in and of the world. To be a woman poet in our society is a double-bind situation, one of conflict and strain. For the words "woman" and "poet" denote opposite and contradictory qualities and roles. Traditionally, the poet is a man, and "poetry" is the poems that men write. The long history of Western literature makes this point painfully clear. It is men who make art, who make books; women make babies. "Women" are, according to society's rules, very different from "poets."

A woman's identity is not defined by a profession, such as poet, but by her personal relationships as daughter, sister, wife, mother. Her "life" is family life. Her art (if she presumes to have one) must necessarily conflict with her life. Usually she is pressured, or pressures herself (for most people are nicely socialized and do not need to be told these rules, having internalized them well), to make a choice: "woman" or "poet."

Is the difference that extreme? Poets are, after all, the least stereotypically masculine of men, in that they are sensitive, emotive, empathetic, intuitive—all traditionally feminine characteristics that, while making women very good at caring about and taking care of people, help men who possess them to be artists. At the same time, poets as a group possess in abundance that primary male attribute, the ego. It takes a strong ego to send out one's work, be rejected, send it out again. But even more profoundly, it takes an enormous ego to say: My experience of the world, my vision of the world, are worth—*I* am worth—your attention. What I say is important! Women traditionally lack not only that self-confidence but that sense of self. Always defined in terms of someone else—someone's daughter, wife, mother—they find their worth, meaning, validity in terms of other people. Consequently, "feminine" women are nurturing and giving, sensitive and committed to interpersonal relations: all to my mind admirable qualities. But in conflict with the role of poet who puts art (and himself) before everything. Selfless versus selfish.

The few existing psychological studies of creative women, on the other hand, show them possessing some "masculine" traits that normal women lack. A pattern of "goal-directed effort" along with "masculine" attitudes appropriate to professional work, such as identification in work and autonomy, appears.[1] Creative women seem to be more original, intelligent, and have a stronger need for accomplishment. In other words, they seem to show more so-called masculine characteristics in those areas that enable them to *produce* creative work: ego strength, independence, need for achievement. If anything, they are suprafeminine in other areas, namely those that would enable them to *be* creative: emotionality, sensitivity, and the rest.

The woman who wants to be a poet, therefore, needs to exhibit certain aspects of herself that her society will label masculine. She is in a double-bind situation, because she is set up to lose, whatever she might do. The conflict between her two "selves" is an excruciating and irreconcilable civil war, when both sides are in fact the same person.

If she is "woman," she must fail as "poet"; "poet," she must fail as "woman." Yet she is not two people. She is a woman poet whose art is a response to, results from, her life. When we explore the developing tradition of poetry by women in twentieth-century America, we observe women who are poets using various tactics to deal with and to struggle against the strain of the double bind in which they find themselves.

Women's poetry is special if only because it comes out of this peculiar tension in their lives as artists. The power of that tension must be recognized, for it can lead to destruction as well as creation and too frequently has done so. Madness is a constant specter and too familiar presence. Two of the nine poets discussed in this book have killed themselves. In each instance, the woman's madness and ultimate suicide seem integrally linked to the conflict and strain experienced in trying to be both woman and artist. To be able to live at all and be a poet seems at times the nearest victory.

If and when a woman chooses to be poet, the double bind exists within the writing itself. Her models have all been men; her criteria and standards of excellence have been created by men describing the work of men. Because the masculine has always been the norm in our society, familiarity with the nature of masculine expression and its formalization in art is long-standing and to a great extent determines our very definitions and evaluations of art. The few women writers who have written and whose names have survived are either thought of as minor artists or have achieved superior status *despite* their womanhood. Yet a woman's experience of the world and manner of experiencing the world (the two are part of one act and cannot be separated) is "feminine," not only when she is menstruating or giving birth but when she is teaching a class or talking to a friend. Whether or not there is any significant biological element affecting the ways in which women think and behave, it is a fact that women in real ways are different from men. They have been brought up to be. Someday there may be no difference, we do not know; but today and throughout our society's history this difference exists. Since poets in Western society are traditionally white and male, a person who is black, or brown, or female of necessity brings qualities different from the norm to the poetry that she or he makes. How, then, to succeed as a "good" poet? If the woman poet "writes like a man," she denies her own experience; if she writes as a woman, her subject matter is trivial.

The development of the new tradition is a history of changing attitudes towards and encounters with this issue. Dickinson at the end of the nineteenth century finds an individual solution that requires private poetry and a private life. Poets until mid-century, like Moore, striving for public recognition, try to live out the split demanded of them between "woman" and "poet"—to play by the boys' rules. This necessitates leaving feminine experience out of art; leaving it at home in the kitchen. By doing so, some women get themselves admitted into the fraternity. By mid-century, however, women poets like Levertov, Plath, and Sexton are beginning to allow this experience into their art. As "feminine" poets, they embody three strategies from a continuum. Levertov, whose work derives most directly from the masculine tradition, frequently needs to abstract and generalize upon the greater significance of an experience to grant it the desired validity. Plath's brief career shows a movement away from a brilliant poetry of surfaces strongly influenced by her male masters to a poetry of engagement and integration between self and world: an art she is creating as she prepares to end her life. Sexton begins where the other two leave off, with an involvement in her own experience of womanhood; she journeys out of private suffering into the public world and role of poet largely by means of the poems that she makes. She, too, however, finds the double bind to be too powerful and kills herself.

Minority women poets are in some ways a separate strand in the tradition's development, because theirs is a triple bind involving race *and* sex oppression. From their overwhelming awareness of race oppression comes the model for political poetry, in which the poet is no longer a writer who "happens" to be black (or happens to be a woman, to translate into feminist terms), but a black poet who writes of, to, for, her or his people—in the language of that people. Among black women poets, Gwendolyn Brooks has made that long journey, although blackness has stayed three steps ahead of womanhood for her. But Brooks has helped make it possible for a younger woman like Giovanni to intertwine blackness and womanhood in a poetry that calls for revolution on both counts. Today, feminist poets are consciously seeking to destroy the double bind itself, to make woman a function of poet, poet a function of woman. Feminist poets like Alta and Adrienne Rich are working to express their own experience in art and find their own forms for expression, that they may discover who they are as women and who they might become. Their voices are very different, precisely because feminine form needs to be an articulation of the person speaking. What they have to say about themselves affects the personal lives of those who read and who hear. The personal and the political unite in this commitment to the self in poetry, in the need to validate the personal and the private as legitimate topics for public speech and in the need to integrate the private and the public worlds. Only in this way can the double bind be broken, can the woman poet be truly one person, an integrated self functioning powerfully in every facet of her experience.

Throughout the century, women have sought to find voices in which they could speak as poets. Some of the difficulty that they have experienced in being heard comes from the strain of trying to make one sound out of two conflicted selves. It is not easy to reach true pitch, to sing and not to gasp or whisper or shout under these conditions. That they have achieved so much is a tribute to their courage, determination, skill, and overwhelming need. This book listens to those voices.

As a feminist literary critic, I employ a specific methodology in writing about the new tradition. I base my assumptions about the work of women poets in my belief that their interactions between self and society are related to the poetry that they write. I see their relationship to one another as occurring in an historical and social context. Yet I am neither psychologist, sociologist, nor historian. I need and call upon knowledge of these disciplines to aid me in studying literary texts, but at the same time my primary focus is those texts. I am concerned with the forms that women poets have created and the themes they have needed to express formally. Therefore, I have chosen particular poets who seem to me to be representative of social and historical moments and motifs, and I have looked closely at the art of these women. I have studied their lives but have discussed biography particularly as it relates to the words that the living woman has written. Primarily, I have read their poetry from the perspective just described and have tried to understand, interpret, and evaluate it out of that perspective. I have neither explained away the poetry as "women's verse," nor have I glorified it because it was written by women, nor have I ignored the sex of the writer as unessential to art. I have tried to read the poems as the work of women poets with sensitivity, intelligence, sympathy, and clarity: to look "naked / at the light," as Adrienne Rich says in her poem "From the Prison House."[2]

NOTES

1. Ravenna Helson, "Personality of women with imaginative and artistic interests: the role of masculinity, originality, and other characteristics in their creativity," *Journal of Personality* 34, no. 1 (March 1966): 22.
2. *Diving into the Wreck* (New York: W. W. Norton, 1973), p. 17.

2

"A Privilege So Awful": The Poetry of Emily Dickinson

"Judge tenderly of me"

When modern American women poets look back to an earlier poet as inspiration or as model, when T. S. Eliot or even William Shakespeare won't do, the name of Emily Dickinson appears. With the exception of Sappho, whose voice comes faint and in fragmentary song over the distance of centuries and cultures, Emily Dickinson is the great woman poet to serve as foremother to a dormant tradition. From Amy Lowell to contemporary poets like Lynn Strongin or myself, poets conscious of themselves as women invoke her name. In "The Sisters" (1925), Amy Lowell writes of Dickinson:

> But Emily hoarded—hoarded—only giving
> Herself to cold, white paper. Starved and tortured,
> She cheated her despair with games of patience
> And fooled herself by winning. Frail little elf,
> The lonely brain-child of a gaunt maturity,
> She hung her womanhood upon a bough
> And played ball with the stars—too long—too long—
> The garment of herself hung on a tree
> Until at last she lost even the desire
> To take it down.[1]

Lynn Strongin's "Emily Dickinson Postage Stamp" was written in 1972:

> No saint on a disc of snow,
> you came back, Emily. Whole,
> into green:
> Not that green which corrupts
> the wave of the brain:
> but a green greater than ocean:
>
> On a stamp,
> hands folded over flowers;
> staring thru all you've lost:
> one love? two love? O host,
> to read a letter, first you'd close the door:
>   Who wrote the world—then heard no more.[2]

My own "The Poems of Women" was written in 1973:

> Tonight I found myself
> furtively dropping poems
> into a red canvas satchel:
>
> poems defacing index cards,
> poems nesting into scraps
> of notebook paper,
> mouse droppings
> crammed into a handbag
> growing rancid
> unread
> hoarded graffiti
> swelling the side of the bag
> like caked powder
> crumbs safety pins
> combs with missing teeth
> bent tampax tubes old addresses
> stray keys to forgotten doors
> stuffed beneath the bed
> among the dustballs.
>
> Emily, you may have had no purse,
> never going anywhere,

never coming downstairs,
eventually.
But every woman needs her pocketbook.
You lived inside yours.[3]

Lowell focuses upon Dickinson's suffering, her solitude, her intellectualism, her heroism, her exile; Strongin emphasizes the relation between Dickinson's present fame and the obscurity she experienced in her own lifetime; I point to the personal, unappreciated and hence private, necessary nature of women's poetry as symbolic extensions of themselves, with Dickinson as the prototype. All three poems treat Dickinson's womanhood as an essential element in her poetry. These poets have an insight born of shared experience into Dickinson as woman poet that has usually been absent from critical evaluation of her. That is, Dickinson's reputation has been based upon either her sex or her poetry, each to the exclusion of the other, with little recognition that she was *both* woman and poet, and that these aspects of herself defined one another.

From 1890, when Mabel Loomis Todd and T. W. Higginson published the first selection of her poetry, *Poems of Emily Dickinson*,[4] until the mid-1930's, when New Critics like Allen Tate, R. P. Blackmur, and John Crowe Ransom took it upon themselves to rescue her poetry and to establish its literary value, Dickinson's reputation was largely founded in biographical interest and speculation. The story of the New England spinster who in her entire lifetime rarely left her father's house, who eventually spent most of her days in her bedroom, who dressed only in white, who scribbled odd little poems onto tiny pieces of paper that she sewed together into packets, whose poems describe seemingly torrid love affairs, caught the romantic imagination of many. Interest centered primarily upon her spinsterhood and her love life. In January 1891, the *Commercial Advertiser* commented in an article titled "Grim Slumber Songs":

> Extreme hunger often causes strange visions. That this hermitess never satisfied, perhaps never could satisfy, her craving for human companionship, may have first brought her into her strangely visionary state. Upon the theme of human love she becomes absurdly, if not blasphemously, intemperate. . . . Isolated from humanity, she cannot turn the current of her thoughts toward it except in intermittent galvanic shocks.

The frustrated-spinster theme (she writes because she is unfulfilled as a woman, but her writing itself suffers from her abnormality) is a common one. "But her poetry? Always as I read it I think of Higginson's impression of her childlikeness. The originality of it is the originality of wondering childhood, and so in its comparisons and analogies."[5] "How monotonous I find her flowers, her bees, and bobolinks . . . how empty her love poems—a love more guessed at than known or wanted. Even the visions of death and eternity . . . seem the product of a curious musing, as though here, too, the point was that experience could be forestalled."[6] The theme continues on into the present; in, for example, a 1961 psychoanalytic study that emphasizes Dickinson's unconscious fear of everything male, caused by the fact that the few males whom she had valued had disappointed her: her father (he did not reciprocate her love), her brother (he married and left her), the critic Higginson (he condescended to her), and even God (he remained silent, beyond her reach).[7] Even when she is being praised, the spinsterly outlook is seen to characterize her work. For example Higginson in 1895 describes her "fine, shy, recluse observation of nature and of men" and compares her work to that of Father Tabb (1845–1909), linking "the celibate woman and the celibate priest."[8]

At the same time, curiosity about her love life, aroused with the publication of the first series ("What Emily Dickinson says of love has a peculiar interest, and it can hardly be forbidden that the reader should wonder what experience of her own she might have had to produce so exceptionally personal utterances"),[9] abounded and resulted in whole series of monographs and biographical volumes that promoted the cause of one or another possible lover, offering for consideration the names of Leonard Humphrey, George Gould, Benjamin Franklin Newton, Charles Wadsworth, Samuel Bowles, Josiah Holland, Otis Lord, and a handsome Irish gardener. The authors of these works, in accepting the greatness of her poetry of love and loss, seem to need to spend their energies in searching for its cause: the underlying assumption being, it seems, that the source of Dickinson's creativity must lie in some man's sexuality.

Both approaches are phallocentric: that (a) Emily Dickinson wrote poetry because she did not have a sex life or (b) the only explanation for such poetry was an active (albeit secret) sex life. Both interpretations lodge the male at the center of a woman's creativity.

In the mid-thirties, the influential trio of New Critics, Tate, Blackmur, and Ransom, contributed to the evaluation of Dickinson as poet from a critical perspective articulated by Blackmur in the following statement:

> The greatness of Emily Dickinson is not . . . going to be found in anybody's idea of greatness, or of Goethe, or intensity, or mysticism, or historical fatality. It is going to be found in the words she used and in the way she put them together; which we will observe . . . as a series of facts about words.[10]

Yet when even these "objective" critics forsake the business of strict textual analysis, we are back with Emily Dickinson, Spinster. Blackmur concludes his contextual studies of the words "plush" and "purple" with this "fact":

> I think it a fact that the failure and success of Emily Dickinson's poetry were uniformly accidental largely because of the private and eccentric nature of her relation to the business of poetry. She was neither a professional poet nor an amateur; she was a private poet who wrote indefatigably as other women cook or knit. Her gift for words and the cultural predicament of her time drove her to poetry instead of antimacassars. Neither her personal education nor the habit of her society as she knew it ever gave her the least inkling that poetry is a rational and objective art and most so when the theme is self-expression.[11]

I think the fact that Dickinson was a woman poet is at the source of both her life-style and her literary style. I see her movement into her house and then her room as paralleling the movement into her mind that her poems document, because both actions were undertaken for the purpose of maintaining her self against pressures from the world to lose it. To explain this notion of keeping or of losing the self, it might be useful to think for a moment not about what she did, but about what she did not do. That is, what her alternatives were, given the time and place and class into which she was born and her knowledge of her own gift. Her alternative was to behave as a "normal" woman: to marry (no doubt someone professional, wealthy, important), to bear children, to manage a house. Where and when would this life-style have given her time and space for her self? The quality of the verse she produced indicates that for her the "meaning" of an experience lay not in an action alone but in her response to it—what she thought about it, what she did with it. There could have been neither time nor space in the life to which the lively, popular, and attractive young Emily

Dickinson was bred for the necessary "recollecting in tranquility" to which poets before her had laid claim. Her own words on the subject are helpful. In her poem about the usual course of events, "She rose to his requirement," the woman described drops the "Playthings of her Life" and takes on the "honorable Work of Woman, and of Wife":

> If ought She missed in Her new Day,
> Of Amplitude, or Awe—
> Or first Prospective—Or the Gold
> In using, wear away,
>
> It lay unmentioned—as the Sea
> Develop Pearl, and Weed,
> But only to Himself—be known
> The Fathoms they abide—[12]

"Amplitude," "Awe," "first Prospective"—this is Dickinson's unique vocabulary, which can be translated into more familiar metaphors such as depth, breadth, vision, meaning. These attributes are missing from the married life of the young woman—and silently mourned. Only deep within herself, however; for even married women soon learn the necessity of keeping themselves to themselves, as much as is possible.

In another poem, "They shut me up in Prose—" (613), she compares her need for the freedom to think to the "stillness" of captivity ("Could they themselves have peeped— / And seen my Brain—go round— / They might as wise have lodged a Bird / For Treason—in the Pound") and refers to a childhood experience that directly relates the socialization of and expectations for girls to the issue:

> As when a little Girl
> They put me in the Closet—
> Because they liked me "still"—

She concludes the poem with a reference to the power of the mind (the comparison to the bird's inherent and uncorruptible wildness persists) to win its freedom, if not literally, then always in spirit:

> Himself has but to will
> And easy as a Star
> Abolish his Captivity—
> And laugh—No more have I—

The cloistered life may be seclusion, but it need not be captivity.

Finally, in an ironic poem in which she is overtly extolling the virtues of passivity, she defines her vision of the poet (who is yet her self, as she is, after all, writing the poem) in a pointedly sex-linked vocabulary of power versus impotence, with the poet and the masculine linked:

> Nor would I be a Poet—
> It's finer—own the Ear—
> Enamored—impotent—content—
> The Licence to revere,
> A privilege so awful
> What would the Dower be,
> Had I the Art to stun myself
> With Bolts of Melody!
>
> (505)

The stanza and its irony are complex, for yet other elements of its vocabulary make it clear that the poet might be a woman who would, however, achieve such a state at great cost—"What would the Dower be"? This would be a different kind of marriage. "Had I the Art to stun myself": Dickinson ends the poem by postulating a situation in which she is both writer and reader, complete in herself but nonetheless alone. Although these lines are hypothetical, in the subjunctive mood, they refer directly to what was indeed her actual situation and point to the price she paid for power, for such "awful" privilege—frightening but also inspiring of greatest awe—that of being a poet.

The "choice" between "artist" and "woman" is one that is not unique to Emily Dickinson: it is that same choice that our society has asked and continues to ask of every woman ambitious for the fame or power or wealth that the world traditionally accords to men. Most women choose to be "women": they remember, perhaps, the days of their youthful hopes for "Amplitude, or Awe"; they perhaps continue to dabble, perpetual amateurs. Of the few who have become artists and won the world's recognition, most have chosen as did Dickinson, sacrificing the traditional "feminine" role of wife and, most certainly, of mother. Yet Dickinson enacted the choice in an especially exaggerated mode. Not all women artists, after all, resort to seclusion in their homes and the wearing of white. Yet it may be argued that Emily Dickinson's situation was more exaggerated than that of most. She was, as most are not, a genius, and the enormous quality of her mind was at violent odds with a particularly conservative social milieu. Thus Dickinson devises a life that will enable her to be a woman poet on her own terms: rejecting the life for which society had prepared her, choosing the life of the mind.

"I dwell in Possibility"

What does it mean to live in the mind? Richness and risk, Dickinson's poems make this clear. She most frequently uses spatial metaphors, especially of chambers and of houses, to describe soul, brain, heart; it is clear from a large number of poems in her canon that she considers these as occupied space.

> The Soul selects her own Society–
> Then–shuts the Door–
> To her divine Majority–
> Present no more–
>
> (303)

> I fear me this–is Loneliness–
> The Maker of the soul
> Its Caverns and its Corridors
> Illuminate–or seal–
>
> (777)

> I dwell in Possibility–
> A fairer House than Prose–
> More numerous of Windows–
> Superior–for Doors–
>
> (657)

> One need not be a Chamber–to be Haunted–
> One need not be a House–
> The Brain has Corridors–surpassing
> Material Place–
>
> (670)

The mental "house" is, if anything, vaster, grander, more impressive than any New England mansion. But these quotations also indicate there are both pros and cons involved in occupying such a space. Solitude leads to the truest insight:

> The Soul's Superior instants
> Occur to Her—alone—
> When friend—and Earth's occasion
> Have infinite withdrawn—
>
> (306)

> Exhilaration—is within—
> There can be no Outer Wine
> So royally intoxicate
> As that diviner Brand
>
> The Soul achieves—Herself—
>
> (383)

Freed from "Earth's occasion," the soul (or mind, these are interchangeable terms) can achieve an exhilaration of spirit that is intoxicatingly powerful. But such a life contains as well profound loneliness—a special kind of terror, which is that of the self observing the self:

> The Loneliness whose worst alarm
> Is lest itself should see—
> And perish from before itself
> For just a scrutiny—
>
> (777)

> Ourself behind ourself, concealed—
> Should startle most—
>
> (670)

When the mind turns its vision upon itself, there is no place to hide.

Yet whether that inner space appears a prison or a sanctuary ("Captivity is Consciousness— / So's Liberty—" [384]), it is real in its own terms and not as analogue for the external. Metaphors of physical space may be used to define its characteristics, but equally are the conceptions of the abstract employed to suggest its perimeters.

> To own the Art within the Soul
> The Soul to entertain

With Silence as a Company
And Festival maintain

Is an unfurnished Circumstance
Possession is to One
As an Estate perpetual
Or a reduceless Mine.

(855)

The surefooted movement in this poem between abstract and concrete through the agency of metaphor is the special dance that characterizes Dickinson's poetic language throughout her work. In these poems about the very place of poetry, its workshop, such relationships are particularly essential to establish. The space of the mind *is* the setting where abstract and concrete exist in reciprocity, each defining the other. "Silence" as a "Company," "Circumstance" being "unfurnished": concepts are granted physicality here. An "Estate" that can be "perpetual," a "Mine" that is "reduceless": physical objects are abstracted into noncorporeality. The space of Dickinson's poetry is the mind's space, and it is created before our eyes by a poetic language dependent upon figures of speech that grant physical immediacy to abstractions and conceptual dimensions to objects.

It is essential, as the poems I have quoted indicate, that Dickinson *define* that inner space with her poetry, for with words she can know what she knows, can see (and tell) where it is that she in fact is. The concluding line of the following poem explains in her characteristically cryptic phrasing the necessary near-paradoxical relation between concrete and abstract that must exist there for her.

There is a solitude of space
A solitude of sea
A solitude of death, but these
Society shall be
Compared with that profounder site
That polar privacy
A soul admitted to itself—
Finite infinity.

(1695)

" 'Nature' is what we see"

If Emily Dickinson lived in the mind, how can she be the poet of "flowers, bees, and bobolinks," the famed observer of the New England landscape?

"Nature" is what we see—
The Hill—the Afternoon—
Squirrel—Eclipse—the Bumble bee—
Nay—Nature is Heaven—
Nature is what we hear—
The Bobolink—the Sea—
Thunder—the Cricket—
Nay—Nature is Harmony—
Nature is what we know—
Yet have no art to say—
So impotent Our Wisdom is
To her Simplicity.

(668)

Nature is what Dickinson experiences with her physical senses: what she sees, hears, knows. But it is as well, as the poem declares, "Heaven," "Harmony," "Simplicity." Nature is the physical embodiment of the unseen but nonetheless real ideas and emotions that populate the mind as robins populate the trees.

The Outer—from the Inner
Derives its Magnitude—
Tis Duke, or Dwarf, according
As is the Central Mood—

(451)

We need our senses, according to Dickinson, to know what we know in tangible form: our knowledge is dependent upon sensory experience for reification, clarification, and, finally, existence itself, for without the senses there is no life, and death extinguishes the mind as well as the body.

Dickinson's "nature poems" are of necessity always about ideas as well as things, about mind as well as matter: they are always about the intricate relation between these aspects of existence, as the following two poems exemplify.

As imperceptibly as Grief
The Summer lapsed away—
Too imperceptible at last
To seem like Perfidy—
A Quietness distilled
As Twilight long begun,
Or Nature spending with herself
Sequestered Afternoon—
The Dusk drew earlier in—
The Morning foreign shone—
A courteous, yet harrowing Grace,
As Guest, that would be gone—
And thus, without a Wing
Or service of a Keel
Our Summer made her light escape
Into the Beautiful.

(1540)

To make a prairie it takes a clover and one bee,
One clover, and a bee,
and revery.
The revery alone will do,
If bees are few.

(1755)

The first poem is about the waning, the "lapsing" of summer. The process is so slow as to be "imperceptible" and has, therefore, a special essence that the poem tries to express. The poem is a series of comparisons: a process in nature is compared to grief, perfidy, quietness, twilight, to Nature spending a secluded afternoon alone with herself; stages of the process are compared to grace, guests, birds, and boats. Since the process by which summer wanes is seen as fundamentally imperceptible, the sequence of comparisons links it with more obvious or more well-known or more understandable processes. It is an ancient and honorable theory of figurative language. For example, Hugh Blair, in his *Lectures on Rhetoric*, in 1762, writes that the purpose of figure is to "render the impression more strong and vivid," especially by assigning the name of some "sensible object" to some "mental object," "giving us frequently a much clearer and more striking view of the principal object."[13] Thus Dickinson begins poems with observations such as "The Past is a curious Creature . . ."; "Prayer is the little implement . . ."; "Death is like the insect . . ."; "Death is a Dialogue . . ."; "The Brain—is wider than the Sky. . . ." The poem in question, however (and many other of her poems), although working from the same principle of figure, seems to be working backwards. Physical things are being compared to "mental objects," concepts, to give them clarity. The process whereby summer lapses is compared to the process whereby grief in humans wanes, its very reticence in going making it, therefore, not treacherous, perfidious. "Grief" and "Perfidy" "flesh out" summer in the poem. It is almost as if they are the physical, the "sensible" objects, not summer, because they, the mind's concepts, are here the more directly knowable. This impression is reinforced in the second stanza, in which the comparisons continue. The lapsing of summer is also like a quietness distilled. Now yet another concept "Quietness," especially by being depicted as "distilled," is given a kind of physicality by which we can perceive that not only is the process in question a lengthy one but one that achieves by its very slowness a rareness of essence, as if, for example, observed in "Twilight long begun," coming upon one, as it were, without notice. The comparison has become most intricate. A process in nature, a physical phenomenon abstracted (the lapsing of summer), is compared to an abstraction, physicalized (quietness distilled), which in turn is explained through a comparison to physical nature (twilight long begun). In turn, the imperceptible process of the lapsing of summer is compared to itself, to nature, but to Nature personified (given the physical body of a human instead of its own physicality), spending a sequestered—secluded, isolated, rare, unique—moment alone with herself: at such a moment she becomes the quintessence of herself.

The poem telescopes the stages of this extended natural event into the "season" of a single day, its twilight and afternoon. The following lines describe the drawings in of its dusk ("earlier") and the shining of its morning ("foreign"). Comparisons continue to draw complex threads of relation between abstract and concrete, inanimate and animate. The strange brightness of this morning's sunlight is explained by a concept, "Grace," personified as courteous yet harrowing, a quality that can best be understood through comparison to a certain kind of person, a "Guest who would be gone."

At last, in the final lines, Summer herself (personified) flies off, yet devoid of corporeality (*no* wings, *no* keel), entering into sheer abstraction, into "the Beautiful." Whatever, wherever, the Beautiful is, the poem has sought to define it for us. The Beautiful has elements of grief but not perfidy, quietness, privacy, brightness and lightness, and a strangeness that is frightening, harrowing, in its courtesy. It exists beyond nature, although composed of nature: it is the very essence of nature (a phrase that also links in intimacy the abstract and the physical: "essence" and "nature"). The poem is a movement between "imperceptible" and "Beautiful"; it explains how total abstraction, which need be, on one level, imperceptible, might be perceived.

In this poem, complex human concepts are linked in a relation with complex moments in the natural world through the physicalization, or "domestication," of abstractions. I say "domestication" because frequently we sense in a Dickinson poem that this use of abstractions in figure comes from extreme familiarity with them, with observing them, that makes them as familiar (as known, experienced *things*) as the phenomena in nature with which the poet is so intimate.

The same principle informs the second short poem. Clovers, bees, and revery are surely on equal footing here, as is again the case in one of my favorite Dickinson couplets, "If summer were an axiom, / What sorcery had snow?" The poem's "meaning" comes from its surefooted movement between "summer," "axiom," "sorcery," and "snow," giving an equality of stature, of concreteness, to words that usually exist on four different levels of abstractness.

In other poems, poems not "about" nature but "about" Emily (poems that begin "I had been hungry, all the Years— / My Noon had Come— to dine"; "I felt a Funeral, in my Brain, / And Mourners to and fro"), Dickinson "objectifies" her personal life through comparisons that link private emotional phenomena and natural objects. But she objectifies them in a special way, for her poetry is always personal, always intimate. The familiarity that gives rise to her "Burglar, banker, father" relationship with God Himself is an extension of her relations with nature and with ideas; she lives with all of these in intimacy.

"Rowing in Eden"

To command her own self is, then, the necessary condition for Dickinson to be a poet. Hence her rejection of woman's traditional roles, hence her seclusion on both a physical and an intellectual plane.

Yet the greatness of her poetry is characterized as much by its fascination with those forces that can annihilate self as by its self-control. Love and death are the primary of these forces: both "Ecstasy" and "Eternity" dissolve self-consciousness in their own state of timelessness, formlessness, and total abstractness. The self, on the other hand, must be tied to time (form) and the senses (pain) in order to live and to experience life.

> Power is only Pain—
> Stranded, thro' Discipline,
> Till Weights—will hang—
> (252)

Dickinson's method, in her poetry of love and death, is to continually approach, describe alluring formlessness with form, which itself safeguards her from losing herself in the process. Her word for this process is "Circumference": through circling to delineate essence.

> When Bells stop ringing—Church—begins—
> The Positive—of Bells—
> When Cogs—stop—that's Circumference—
> The Ultimate—of Wheels.
> (633)

Her love poetry is famous for its sensitivity, its insight into the nuances of feeling, ever-changing yet always intense, that comprise the situation called love. It is obvious from these poems that Emily Dickinson experienced love: whether it was on the couch in her parlor or in the confines of her imagination is not an especially important issue. She knows what she writes about, and she transfers her experience and her understanding of that experience into language as few poets before or since have done. (Her talent is always for probing an emotion or state of mind, distilling its essence; in explaining it, not uncomplicating it, but rather expanding its profundity with words: circumference.) Yet though their moods are myriad, there is a theme that colors many of these poems: the necessity of sacrifice, or rather abstinence; the acceptance of the pain that is love accompanied by a reluctance to know its joy.

> It might be lonelier
> Without the Loneliness—

I'm so accustomed to my Fate—
Perhaps the Other—Peace—

Would interrupt the Dark—
And crowd the little Room—
Too scant—by Cubits—to contain
The Sacrament—of Him—

I am not used to Hope—
It might intrude upon—
Its sweet parade—blaspheme the place—
Ordained to Suffering—

It might be easier
To fail—with Land in Sight—
Than gain—My Blue Peninsula—
To perish of Delight—

(405)

A longer poem begins:

I cannot live with You—
It would be Life—
And Life is over there—
Behind the Shelf

The Sexton keeps the Key to—

It ends:

So We must meet apart—
You there—I—here—
With just the Door ajar
That Oceans are—and Prayer—
And that White Sustenance—
Despair—

(640)

Although a variety of metaphoric equivalences are found to describe the distance between her present tense of pain and a possible or future union with the beloved in bliss, the most common vocabulary employed is that of sea and ships. It occurs in the poems just quoted. In the first, in the final stanza, the suffering poet is at sea. To hope to reach her beloved would be to gain her "Blue Peninsula": but on such a shore she would surely, she believes, "perish of Delight"—die of love. It might be easier, then, to "fail—with Land in Sight"—to stay in the place "Ordained to Suffering." In the concluding stanzas of "I cannot live with You," the sea again appears in a more complex figure, which in Dickinson fashion mingles abstract and concrete with dexterity in order to approach the feeling experienced. The distance between the lovers is as small ("just the Door ajar") as "Oceans are" (small in miles, perhaps; deep and wide and limitless in feeling). This distance is equated with oceans, prayer, and a "White Sustenance—Despair." A conceptual distance is first compared to a concrete space, oceans, then to another concept, prayer, and finally to a concept made concrete: despair as a white food. Experiencing the distance between them, in its pain and possibility, is yet experiencing the love between them, the poet says. One can live on it.

The existence of and even need for a space between the lovers is further clarified in the poem that follows.

> You left me—Sire—two legacies—
> A Legacy of Love
> A Heavenly Father would suffice
> Had He the offer of—
>
> You left me Boundaries of Pain—
> Capacious as the Sea—
> Between Eternity and Time—
> Your Consciousness—and Me—
>
> (644)

The power of the poem is in the final stanza, the one devoted not to love but to its pain. Again the sea is used as a fitting analogue to the experience of pain—here, specifically, its spaciousness. The final lines define the shores of that sea: on one side, the lover ("Your Consciousness"), on the other, the poet ("Me"); on one side, eternity, on the other, time. The parallel structure of the lines links lover and eternity, poet and time. He is on the far shore, she on the near; to reach him would be to overcome time and arrive in eternity. This poem specifically equates two unreachable goals, fulfilled love and achieved death.

The sea imagery usually has sexual implications that help the reader to understand more clearly why fulfillment has to be unattainable. In the next poem, the lover is the port, and the experience of love is the tumultuous sea.

> Wild Nights—Wild Nights!
> Were I with thee
> Wild Nights should be
> Our luxury!
>
> Futile—the Winds—
> To a Heart in port—
> Done with the Compass—
> Done with the Chart!
>
> Rowing in Eden—
> Ah, the Sea!
> Might I but moor—Tonight—
> In Thee!
>
> (249)

This is a poem of passion, where the storm of the physical world becomes an analogue for the sexual throes—which are, however, only imagined in the poem, a subjunctive possibility ("Were I with thee"). Yet a further comparison is made: the sea (of love) in storm is "Eden" itself—a paradise sea now denied to fallen humanity (in a state of pain, and time), rich with sea-blossoms, sea-fruits. "Rowing in Eden," with its chaste vocabulary, is one of the most sensual lines in literature.

The self-denied goal may be the further shore, the lover, bliss; but her images at times also connect the sea itself with him, because it is allied with passion and therefore loss of self.

> The Drop, that wrestles in the Sea—
> Forgets her own locality—
> As I—toward Thee—
>
> (284)

> Least Rivers—docile to some sea.
> My Caspian—thee.
>
> (212)

Drowning—death—passion—death—heaven—death—paradise—death: the the death of love is the loss of self.

> Come slowly—Eden!
> Lips unused to Thee—
> Bashful—sip thy Jessamines—
> As the fainting Bee—
>
> Reaching late his flower,
> Round her chamber hums—
> Counts his nectars—
> Enters—and is lost in Balms.
> (211)

Here, in one of Dickinson's most erotic poems, passion as paradise is the basis for an extended metaphor in which the sexual act is compared to the encounter of bee with flower. Eden as garden is emphasized here, but the conclusion is the same as in all of the other poems quoted: the bee is "lost in Balms." The overwhelming fragrance (or oil) is akin to the sea; in it one drowns and is "lost." Although the poem begins with a cautious yet hopeful attitude (go slow, I'm not used to this, I've waited a long, long time), its climax is ambiguous: wonderful yet deadly.

It seems apparent from the evidence of her poetry that Emily Dickinson did not run off with Judge Lord or Charles Wadsworth or the handsome Irish gardener solely for reasons of impropriety or maidenly delicacy or even fear; she had as well reasons of self-defense that many modern feminists have advocated. That she did explore the fruits of passion her poems make clear, but the space in which it happened was the space of poetry, carefully circumscribed and controlled by her own power with words.

"I could not see to see"

That other dangerous force attracting Dickinson from her seclusion is death. Not the physical process of dying itself so much as what that represents: the attainment of what is variously called in her poems "Heaven" or "Eternity." Where the dead go is what interests her. And, even more importantly, once "there," what do they know? Her fascination with death is not macabre, as some have labeled it; it is the desire of the finite for the infinite, the yearning of consciousness for that moment of total expansion—before, just as unconsciousness sets in. Of the fact that unconsciousness must, ultimately, set in there is little doubt in her mind. That is why and where Dickinson and a poet like Plath (also passionately interested in death) part ways. For Dickinson "plays" at death in her poetry, experiences it over and over in imagination, just because she is safe there from losing control of herself, whereas Plath uses her poetry as a preparation for her death. (It is not that Plath is unable to distinguish between art and life, but that she as "rebel" attempts to link them as Dickinson never tries to do. Dickinson chooses to live in the mind—in art; Plath tries to have both art and a woman's "life"—and fails.)

In many poems, from a myriad of perspectives (circumference), Dickinson describes herself as dead. She pictures herself in the grave, with "granite lip" (182), driving civilly along with Death in a carriage (712), or encountering the horror of Death, its "Face of Steel," "metallic grin": "The Cordiality of Death— / Who drills his Welcome in—" (286). She describes herself in the very act of dying, having willed her keepsakes, with her relatives gathered round ready for the end, hearing a fly buzz:

> . . . and then it was
> There interposed a Fly—
>
> With Blue—uncertain stumbling Buzz—
> Between the light—and me—
> And then the Windows failed—and then
> I could not see to see—
>
> (465)

There is no way to continue, or to end, this poem that deals with physical death. After the relatives and the prayers and the wills, what is left, signifying the whole world for the poet, is one uncertainly buzzing fly. Perception of the fly proves that she still can hear, see: it is where all meaning now lies. But then her senses fail. That is, she knows they must fail, but she cannot imagine her own lack of consciousness. The poem's final line is so marvelous because of that;

because she is still seeing that she is not able to see. The light does not go out.

In other, more subtle poems, death becomes a metaphor for itself. In "I felt a Funeral in my Brain" (280), the dead person (the poet) transfers the funeral activities to the inside of her brain, experiencing them in that inner space of existence familiar to the reader of Dickinson's poems. The mourners tread; the service, "like a Drum," beats: the vibrations are so strong it seems that "Sense" is "breaking through" or that her "Mind" is "going numb." Her consciousness hovers between real life and final death. But of course the speaker of the poem is dead—the consciousness that she cannot help but manifest is imagined (even as the consciousness is real and the death is imagined). This intricate set of transfers is what initiates the poem's situational transfer, in which the funeral service is held within the mind.

Next the speaker hears a box (her coffin) being lifted, hears it "creak" across her soul. Then (after the burial) all reverses, and inner space opens wide into outer space. The poet encounters eternity:

> Then Space—began to toll,
>
> As all the Heavens were a Bell,
> And Being, but an Ear,
> And I, and Silence, some strange Race
> Wrecked, solitary, here—
>
> And then a Plank in Reason, broke,
> And I dropped down, and down—
> And hit a World, at every plunge,
> And Finished knowing—then—

The sounds of her funeral, its treading and beating and creaking, expand into the sound of space itself, the profound rhythmical pulsing that is the life force and the death knell, as all the heavens become a bell, and being is transformed into the ear that hears its beat. But the poet must equate herself with silence, not being (together some strange race, because for them the sound is growing, has grown weak). She is alone and "wrecked"—washed ashore from that sea upon which she continually portrays herself as sailing, that sea which is pain and torment and storm, which is life. Once again concepts are physicalized

("Space—began to toll"), objects abstracted ("I, and Silence, some strange Race") at an alarming rate. The final lines of the poem insist that the space she now inhabits is neither inner space as metaphor for outer space, nor outer space as metaphor for inner space, but both together, for they are one in the end. For, in the final moments of the poem, the fall into loss of consciousness takes place when a plank in reason (the floor on which she stands, the floor of the brain) finally breaks (from the force of all that beating and treading, those boots of lead, surely), and she plummets endlessly, hitting worlds at every plunge (falling through outer space, eternity) until she must stop knowing. . . . Yet the poem ends with a conjecture, and a dash, a gasp: the poem stops just before the fact (even as does "I heard a Fly buzz—when I died—"), because there can be no more poems after the "then" with which this poem stops.

Eternity is absolute abstraction, something the mind can approach through circumference but can never know. Eternity is that place where summer goes in "As imperceptibly as Grief"—into the Beautiful: essence, or total abstraction. Poetry itself comes closest of all human devices to knowing it, simply because the forms of poetry can "pretend" at formlessness, can hypothesize it and approximate it with the figurative possibilities of language that do not occur in nature: can encounter abstract and concrete in the same space, in a place where their qualities interact for the purposes of definition, elucidation, revelation.

As if the Sea should part
And show a further Sea—
And that—a further—and the Three
But a presumption be—

Of Periods of Seas—
Unvisited of Shores—
Themselves the Verge of Seas to be—
Eternity—is Those—

(695)

The movement in this poem of definition from concrete to greater and greater abstraction in order to attempt comprehension—to come to the borders of the ultimate abstraction, eternity—must be understood in the context of its symbolic basis. The Sea with which it begins is at once literal sea and that symbolic sea of life that so frequently crashes in

Dickinson's poetry. A concept, in other words, is physicalized in order to be deliberately abstracted again: the method of circumference.

The complete poem occurs in the subjunctive mood (that space which is "contrary to fact," mental space): "as if." To understand eternity, we need to *imagine* that the sea (the literal sea of ships and sharks) might part and reveal beyond itself a further sea, and beyond that sea, one further yet; and all three themselves be "but a presumption." . . . A double, triple? conceptualization, where the subjunctive or imagined literal sea, which in parting becomes gradually more abstract, is revealed to be itself conjecture: a movement from the sea to Sea to presumption—sailing boldly on the seas of abstraction. The presumption is "of Periods of Seas": of the idea of seas, the Platonic Idea. And *if* this conjectured concept, such "Unvisited of Shores," were itself but the edge of further unknown, uncomprehended seas, then those seas would be that space we seek to understand because it exists always at the defining edge of our own consciousness, our own lives—eternity. Dickinson's simple vocabulary, her clear, uncomplicated rhythms, express a mental exercise that itself is almost beyond the bounds of comprehension.

"To be alive—is Power"

Emily Dickinson did not, except in imagination, give herself up to love or death. That is, she did not assume the traditional woman's role of wife and mother that has for its justification and *raison d'être* the power and necessity of love for women; she did not give in to the power of death, which in practical terms means suicide—a traditional method of ending the conflict that women artists experience between the stressful role demands of woman and artist. Her power of mind was great enough to enable her to handle both impulses safely—to use poetry itself as the agent of experience. At times she must have yearned for the "normal" life of the women she knew and cared about; it is impossible to escape one's socialization and the influence of society completely. Her poems express this feeling, too.

> A Door just opened on a street—
> I—lost—was passing by—
> An instant's Width of Warmth disclosed—
> And Wealth—and Company.

The Door as instant shut—And I—
I—lost—was passing by—
Lost doubly—but by contrast—most—
Informing—misery—

(953)

Yet she seems to have understood and to have dealt with the problem of being a woman poet in a more triumphant way than most before or since, and I think this is because her poetry—and the mind that could conceive of it and conceive it—was so unusually great. Most of the time, as her poetry indicates, she does not feel a sense of loss, does not feel left out of life. On the contrary, she feels that she is vitally involved in life.

To be alive—is Power—
Existence—in itself—
Without a further function—
Omnipotence—Enough—

To be alive—and Will!
'Tis able as a God—
The Maker—of Ourselves—be what—
Such being Finitude!

(677)

The prime purpose of, and test of, life is to create oneself. The person who can do this is all-powerful, omnipotent. (Most women never do get to this point: forever defined in terms of someone else—"Frau Doktor. Frau Architect. Mrs. George Blank. Mrs. Harry Blank"—they "can't leave the room without a big wooden pass."[14]) When one is properly created, properly oneself, one is—as her poems indicate—in a position of power over nature itself.

Perhaps I asked too large—
I take—no less than skies—
For Earths, grow thick as
Berries, in my native town—

My Basket holds—just—Firmaments—
Those—dangle easy—on my arm,
But smaller bundles—Cram.

(352)

By using the housewife's own vocabulary, Dickinson gently mocks the traditional woman's restricted life and self in comparison with her own. Her "native town" is the mind, that version of woman's inner space that is as profound and expansive as the psychologist Erik Erikson's use of the term is reductive, restrictive.[15] Once again, this poem points to the nature of that expansivenes by its conception of the meaning of space itself. Inner space includes within its perimeters outer space: "For Earths, grow thick as / Berries, in my native town." "Berries" is the word from nature that helps us understand the similarities, and the differences, between round objects, between berries in literal towns and earths in imaginative towns, or imaginary earths in imaginary towns, or earths in the town of the imagination. The space of the mind is great enough to contain "just" firmaments; they dangle easily in her mental basket, while "smaller bundles"—the trivia of the existence of the so-called fulfilled woman—cram.

Even those of us today who take our feminism to mean that we must no longer make the choice between mind and body that society has demanded of us need Emily Dickinson as a source of strength. Sitting in the world of her room, of her mind, she understood the issues—their dangers and their potential victories—and expressed them for us with profound clarity.

NOTES

1. Florence Howe and Ellen Bass, eds., *No More Masks: An Anthology of Poems by Women* (New York: Anchor Press, 1973), pp. 43–44.
2. Ibid., p. 274.
3. Nancy E. James, ed., *I, That Am Ever Stranger: Poems on Women's Experience* (New Wilmington, Pennsylvania: Globe Printing Co., 1974), p. 55.
4. Mabel Loomis Todd and T. W. Higginson, eds., *Poems of Emily Dickinson* (Boston: Roberts Brothers, 1890).
5. Fred Lewis Pattee, "Gentian, Not Rose: The Real Emily Dickinson," *Sewanee Review* 45 (Spring 1937): 197.
6. G. W. Stonier, "Innocence without Experience," *The New Statesman and Nation* 14 (October 23, 1937): 655.
7. Clark Griffith, "Emily Dickinson's Love Poetry," *Iowa English Yearbook* 6 (Autumn 1961): 15–22.
8. *The Nation*, 23 May 1895.

9. "The Literary Wayside," *Springfield Republican*, December 2, 1894.

10. R. P. Blackmur, "Emily Dickinson: Notes on Prejudice and Fact," *The Southern Review* 3 (Autumn 1937): 325–47.

11. Ibid., pp. 346–47.

12. Thomas H. Johnson, ed., *The Complete Poems of Emily Dickinson* (Boston: Little, Brown and Co., 1960), p. 359 (#732). All other citations to Dickinson's poems are to Johnson's edition and his numerical system.

13. Hugh Blair, *Lectures on Rhetoric and Belles Lettres* (London and Edinburgh, 1813), pp. 198, 203.

14. Erica Jong, "The Artist as Housewife," *Ms.*, December 1972, p. 64.

15. Erik Erikson, "Reflections on Womanhood," in Robert Jay Lifton, ed., *The Woman in America* (Boston: Beacon Press, 1967).

3

"Felicitous Phenomenon": The Poetry of Marianne Moore

The first generation of modern poets in America includes such names as T. S. Eliot, Ezra Pound, William Carlos Williams, Robert Frost, Wallace Stevens, John Crowe Ransom, Archibald MacLeish, E. E. Cummings, Hart Crane, Allen Tate, Robinson Jeffers, H. D., Edna St. Vincent Millay, and Marianne Moore. Who are the great ones? Still in the century, one cannot label with absolute certainty, but some reputations are nearly impregnable now: Eliot, Pound, Williams, Stevens. The women poets are not in that list of masters, but they have nevertheless begun to appear on lists. Women have entered the tradition.

What explains this? Several factors can be isolated. First, the slowly changing role of women in American society. The first wave of American feminism (1840–1920) had achieved neither revolution nor liberation for women, but it had helped bring about some changes: the vote for women (1920), the admission of women into higher education (1865).[1] The latter is of especial importance in relation to the literary dimension of this complex situation. The poetry that was beginning to be written in America and England as the century turned—experimental, radical, "modern"—was the product of university-educated men who had conscious and articulated reasons for rejecting the literary tradition in which they had been educated. All three of the women that belong to the first generation of modern poets went to college. Both H. D. (Hilda

Doolittle) and Marianne Moore were college acquaintances of the men who went on to become the formative figures in the new poetry scene: Pound, Eliot, Williams. Later, H. D. went to London and was associated with that group of poets, meeting before the First World War, whom Pound called Imagists; these included Richard Aldington, whom she married (and later divorced). Marianne Moore was a central figure in the New York literary scene during the same period, meeting in Greenwich Village from 1915 on with artists and editors like Williams, Stevens, Alfred Kreymbourg, Walter Arensberg, Hart Crane, Kenneth Burke, Mina Loy, and E. E. Cummings. In the early twenties, Louis Zukofsky used the term "Objectivism" to characterize the work of many in this group, but always the underlying principles of the modernist movement were similar, with the names for modernist "schools" being more various than the members of the groups. There was, for example, constant communication and interchange between the poets in England and America, with Pound, especially, serving as transatlantic correspondent, sending the poems of Frost, Eliot, Lawrence, H. D., to America, publishing Williams and Amy Lowell in London.

The existence of women in these literary circles has much to do, therefore, with a greater freedom in the society for women to be educated and to take part in professional life. It is also connected, it seems to me, with the nature of the poetic revolution itself, with the new aesthetic that Imagists, Futurists, Vorticists, Objectivists, were working to create and promote.

In response to nineteenth-century Romanticism, to a poetry that seemed at once messily subjective, philosophic, and rhetorical, modern poets stressed the objective, the particular, the precise, the concrete, and the visual. In the March 1913 issue of *Poetry*, there appeared this list of Imagist principles in F. S. Flint's article, "Imagisme":

1. Direct treatment of the "thing," whether subjective or objective.
2. To use absolutely no word that does not contribute to the presentation.
3. As regarding rhythm: to compose in the sequence of the musical phrase, not in the sequence of a metronome.[2]

Yet Pound had defined the image as "an intellectual and emotional complex in an instant of time":[3] "objective" implies the existence, if not the expression, of the subjective; "particular," of the general; "precise," of the imprecise; "concrete," of the abstract; "concise," of the expanded; "visual," of the unseen (as I have pointed out in *Metaphor and the*

Poetry of Williams, Pound, and Stevens).[4] Eliot's definition of the "objective correlative" is really a set of working notes for the creation of this kind of poetry. To express emotion in the form of art, he says, one has to find "a set of objects, a situation, a chain of events which shall be the formula of that *particular emotion*; such that when the external facts, which must terminate in sensory experience, are given, the emotion is immediately evoked."[5]

Eliot's formula indicates that the focus of the modern aesthetics is primarily procedural. Poets remain interested in expressing universal truths, but they have found a different methodology for doing so that seems to them at once more effective and more in tune with their twentieth-century emphasis on the technical (in literary art translated into a concern with technique, with form and style). The methodology is, however, more directly related to what has been traditionally women's domain: the circumscribed, specific, particular. The women associated with the modern movement in poetry were particularly good at this sort of thing. H. D.'s "Oread" is frequently cited as the perfect Imagist poem; Zukofsky recommended Moore's "An Egyptian Pulled Glass Bottle in the Shape of a Fish" as the superior Objectivist poem.[6]

During the first half of the twentieth century, women poets were trying to get into the tradition, not to start their own. Although this fact is understandable, it is also directly related to the nature and quality of their literary achievement. Professional recognition, by poets and critics alike, has a great deal to do with belonging to the club. Being "one of the boys," in the case of Marianne Moore, for example, who was "surely the leading woman in modern American literature,"[7] resulted in a concentration upon technical brilliance coupled with a marked exclusion of feminine experience from art. "Woman" and "poet" were separated as the most effective means of achieving professional success.

Moore may have been the leading American woman poet, but she was not the leading American poet. One reason for her lesser stature is the limited nature of her achievement, a limitation that *is* related to her womanhood: not to the inferiority of women but to their societal status, to the "double bind" of the woman artist. The great works of Eliot, Pound, Williams, and Stevens transcend the original confinements of the Imagist aesthetic in ways that the poetry of Moore never does. They rely heavily on the personal experience of each individual poet as translated into universal truths and generalities. Pound does not have to deny his masculine experience, because it is that of mankind: the *Cantos* make this expressly clear. So do all the major American poetic works from Walt Whitman's *Leaves of Grass* to Charles Olson's *Maximus Poems*. Moore, on the other hand, like most women poets in most ways until mid-century, can safely use only those elements of subjective personal experience that are not specifically sex-linked, and for even these she must find acceptable objective correlatives. She must, in other words, translate her experience into the masculine forms and symbols that are current and correct. She limited herself, but she did so in direct response to her society.

Because Marianne Moore has usually been considered the leading woman in modern American literature, I have used her work as the subject of this essay. I think that her stratagems and successes are representative of women who are poets in the first half of the century, but the fact that this is an ever-expanding group during a lengthy period necessarily qualifies her representational status. The first generation is followed by a second, that of Josephine Miles, Elizabeth Bishop, Gwendolyn Brooks, Louise Bogan, and Muriel Rukeyser. Individual variations on and exceptions to the theme occur, but the theme is there: a neat division between "woman" and "poet," with art and artistry belonging to the domain of the latter.

Indeed, for these poets, "women" are a separate category in both their lives and their work. That is, when they talk about women, they are usually referring to a group other than themselves. Describing a reading of her verse for a women's club, Moore tells the following anecdote:

> After the program, a strikingly well-dressed member of the audience, with equally positive manner, inquired, "What is metaphysical newmown hay?"
>
> I said, "Oh, something like a sudden whiff of fragrance in contrast with the doggedly continuous opposition to spontaneous conversation that had gone before."
>
> "Then why don't you *say* so?" the impressive lady rejoined.[8]

There is an obvious distinction being made here between the poet, who uses language figuratively, gives readings to women's clubs, is herself neither strikingly well-dressed (Moore is famous for her eccentric mode of dress) nor especially self-confident (she later omitted those lines from her poem), and the woman—all that the poet is not, but, as the tone of Moore's remarks makes clear, also not what the poet is. Her long poem "Marriage" is her only work explicitly about a subject directly concerned with women; it is the only poem that anthologies of women poets usually include to represent the most famous modern American woman poet. In "Marriage," "woman" is clearly other than the poet: "Eve: beautiful woman— / I have seen her / when she was so handsome / she gave me a start."[9] Why not, when Marianne Moore the person has made it explicit that such feminine activity has nothing to do with her; that she is in fact superior to such activities: "What of chastity? It confers a particular strength. Until recently, I took it for granted as a universally regarded asset, like avoiding 'all drugs.' "[10]

As poet, Moore stands midway between the solitary Emily Dickinson, whose personal solutions to the demands of her life and art created a poetry that denied neither of those elements but was of necessity a private poetry, even as the life from which it grew was also private, and poets such as Denise Levertov, Sylvia Plath, and Anne Sexton, who in mid-century begin to explore techniques for functioning publicly as artists who can yoke "woman" and "poet." The poetry of Moore and her contemporaries is necessary in order that the women's tradition might develop within the legitimacy of the masculine tradition, but it is characterized as much by denial as by affirmation, by defense more often than attack.

"The passion for setting people right is itself an afflictive disease."

Critical response to Marianne Moore over six decades has affirmed a split between "woman" and "poet." On the one hand, literary criticism rarely deals with the fact of her womanhood (even the frequent comparisons to Dickinson begin at this point of connection in order to discuss technical matters); while on the other hand, a public personality defined by certain kinds of female stereotypes was projected and "appreciated" by her admirers.

The formal discipline and precision of her work called forth critical studies focused on verbal techniques: on structure and style. From the first, the poets themselves, with their heightened interest in such matters, recognized and sought to promote an accomplished fellow craftsman; the tone in literary analysis was set by Eliot, Williams, Pound, and Stevens. Eliot, whose discussions are studded with observations such as "Here the rhythm depends partly upon the transformation changes from one image to another, so that the second image is superimposed before the first has quite faded, and upon the dexterity of change of vocabulary from one image to another," summarizes her worth: "Miss Moore is, I believe, one of those few who have done the language some service during my lifetime."[11] Williams, especially, responded to Moore's use of words with eloquent metaphors of his own in many essays: "Miss Moore gets great pleasure from wiping soiled words or cutting them clean out, removing the aureoles that have been pasted about them or taking them bodily from greasy contexts."[12] That literary philosopher with one of the century's most complex minds, Kenneth Burke, repeatedly found her work grist for his subtle mill.

> . . . the surfaces are derived from depth; indeed, the strict lawfulness in their choice of surfaces is depth. And the objects treated have the property not simply of things, but of volitions. They derive their poignancy as motifs from their relation to the source of motive. And the relation between observer and observed is not that of news and reporter, but of "conversities" (her word).[13]

Later full-length volumes on Moore, such as Bernard Engel's *Marianne Moore* or Donald Hall's *Marianne Moore: The Cage and the Animal*,[14] have linked together readings of poems with thematic or ethical threads, but, on the whole, critical focus understandably follows the lead set by a poetry that foregrounds its own act of work-making and patterning.

What sort of woman was she, the creator of at once hard and exquisite poems looking out with discriminating detail on the rarer species of existence, of a translation of *The Fables of La Fontaine*, and a small body of critical essays? "Marianne Moore . . . a caryatid, her red hair plaited and wound twice about the fine skull . . . Marianne, with her sidelong laugh and shake of the head, quite child-like and overt . . . Marianne was our saint—if we had one—in whom we all instinctively felt our purpose come together to form a stream. Everyone loved her," writes Williams about Moore in the early days.[15] "A beautiful woman wearing the tricorn hat and great cape which then served as customary dress," William Wasserman describes her in 1958.[16] "Marianne Moore is a woman with a narrow head and pale blue eyes which seem to gather all light into them. She is so unfashionable that she seems extremely fashionable."[17] "Then Marianne took over the editorial chair [of the *Dial*] deferently, modestly, but with what firm notions about the English language!"[18] "For many years you charmed us, / And never harmed us."[19]

Born in 1887 in St. Louis, Moore was educated at Bryn Mawr ("I seemed to need very humane handling, mothering by everybody—the case all my life, I think");[20] in 1918 she moved to New York City, where she lived with her mother in Greenwich Village and Brooklyn. She worked half days from 1921 to 1925 in the New York Public Library; from 1925 to 1929 she was editor of the important literary magazine the *Dial*. She traveled once to Europe, in 1911, and crossed the United States four times. She was devoted to baseball. She did not marry. "Well, I think anyone aiming to marry can do it. . . . I'm not matrimonially ambitious."[21] She was and is admired for her intellect, her charm, her skill, her modesty: "What I write, as I have said before, could only be called poetry because there is no other category in which to put it."[22] She was so successful in the literary world because she could at once capitalize on and repress different aspects of her femininity. Her feminine virtues of "deference" and "modesty" and charm were the ones with which men are most comfortable (and flattered); while in opting for nonsexuality, she escaped those feminine characteristics that threaten, especially in a woman who also claims—through intelligence and talent—to be an equal. She did not compete as a woman, although she may have charmed as one. When she writes about the "particular strength" that chastity confers, she writes from direct experience. Chastity is nonengagement; it leaves one in a position of safety. Like so many of the animals upon whom she focused her poetic vision, she adapted to her environment and the problems it posed with a skill that may have been unconscious but was nonetheless profitable.

Occasionally, Moore's status as woman poet is implicitly or even explicitly recognized, as when Roy Harvey Pearce compares her with her male contemporaries:

> There is thus even in the best of Williams, Aiken, and Cummings, a certain chest-pounding bravado which might well conceal a fear of the unknown and unknowable. They so often tend to overreact, to protest much too loudly. Modesty is not one of their virtues; nor, at their best, need it be. Yet at their worst, we so often wish it were. Wit, irony, perspective, a sense of *noblesse oblige* and high-civility, a certain relaxed ease, an easing up on the reins: all this their way of poetry will not let them have. All this Marianne Moore does have. But she pays a certain

> cost, too: at her worst, she is fussy, gossipy, uncertain as to direction and development. Yet at her best she has a sense of propriety which we can only prize.[23]

Pearce is appreciating her womanly virtues in poetry but at the same time finding her limitations to be those of her social role: spinsterly. Charles Tomlinson notes in his introduction to *A Collection of Critical Essays*, "Marianne Moore: Her Poetry and Her Critics," the existence of a "host of 'tributes' in which the poet is reduced to the status of a kind of national pet and where the intellectual stamina finds no answering attitude in the appreciator but calls forth instead sentimental rhapsodizing."[24] He does not link this response to her femininity, as projected by her public self and not by her poetry, but it seems clear to me. Robinson Jeffers observes the glassed-in nature of her poetry, which is a result of the split she has enforced between life and art, although he does not comment upon any possible causes.

> We are uncomfortable—or else too comfortable—in a world in which feeling, affection, charity, are so entirely divorced from sexuality and power, the bonds of the flesh. In this world of the poems there are many thoughts, things, animals, sentiments, moral insights: but money and passion and power, the brute fact that *works*, whether or not correctly, whether or not precisely—the whole Medusa-face of the world: these are gone. . . . Few poets have as much moral insight as Miss Moore; yet in her poems morality usually *is* simplified into self-abnegation, and Gauguin always seems to stay home with his family—which is right, but wrong in a way, too. Poems which celebrate morality choose more between good and evil, and less between lesser evils and greater goods, than life does, so that in them morality is simpler and more beautiful than it is in life, and we feel our attachment to it strengthened.[25]

He is surely alluding to her spinster role, but I think that he is saying less that she couldn't know and more that she has chosen not to know; I agree.

Frequent comparisons to Dickinson recognize, at least initially, her sex; more importantly, though, the poets are seen to share "fastidious precision of thought,"[26] "the dignity of being curt about great things they know. An asceticism in each . . . a trenchant authority with language,"[27] though Moore is "without Emily Dickinson's range and passion."[28] In his essay "Two Philologists" (1969), Henry Gifford with a certain degree of embarrassment tries the "experiment" of comparing the two poets. He bases his efforts in his observation that "no such thing exists as a female tradition in poetry; but there are feminine attributes which a woman poet cannot overlook in herself without falsity."[29] What unites Moore and Dickinson in his analysis is "their choice of language, which is incontrovertibly American. . . . They are individual, ironic, and above all fastidious. They place a high value on privacy and know the power of reticence. Their poetry is exact and curious like the domestic skills of the American woman in ante-bellum days."[30] Yet Gifford notices a difference, too; that the "I" in Moore's poem is not "central and exposed" like the "I" in Dickinson. Rather, it generalizes.[31] In this last comment, Gifford is right on target, although it is for him not a major point, and for most of his essay he concentrates on language matters that his juxtaposition of the two poets has highlighted.

Right on target, because the difference between the "central and exposed self" in Dickinson's poetry and the armored self in Moore's has much to do with the latter's lesser "range and passion." Gifford's observation points to the fact that a surface of precise linguistic concern may have different functions and effects: Dickinson uses poetry as a way and a place to encounter the self, while for Moore the poem is the ultimate defense, the strongest protection. Even as a separation of life from art seems the best tactic for succeeding at both, so in each world a separation of private from public helps to prevent exposure. For these fissures are always figurative, not literal: when one is "poet" the "woman" is not home sewing; she is present but hidden and needs constant protection. Moore's famous "objectivity" seems less a poetic device for connecting observer with observed, observer and observed with audience, than a wall: all those carefully polished words and perfect structures can form an impenetrable barrier.

The "superior objectivist poem," her "An Egyptian Pulled Glass Bottle in the Shape of a Fish," is a poem appreciating art itself according to criteria that can be applied easily to her own poetry. Uncharacteristically, she begins not with the physical details of the fish-bottle but with the practical and moral situation that led to its making. Her poem is tracing the process of creation itself, so that it leads to the presence of the bottle as its conclusion. "Here we have," she begins, observing the bottle, "thirst," "patience," then "art": "as in a wave held up for us to see / in its essential perpendicularity." Art is thus the result of physical need and the skill of the artist to create what is needed: "So art is but an expression of our needs," she writes in her essay "Feeling and Precision"; "is feeling, modified by the writer's moral and technological insights."[32] Art demands appreciation, so the poem's first stanza concludes. Then the second and final stanza goes on to appreciate that which the artist has created:

> not brittle but
> intense—the spectrum, that
>   spectacular and nimble animal the fish,
>   whose scales turn aside the sun's sword by their polish.

The work of art, to paraphrase, is not false but real; "genuine" is her term in another poem of definition, "Poetry." This bottle is more than something that aids in the alleviation of thirst, it is a fish—a fish created more intensely, more perfectly, more essentially than its living model because it is glass. Perfected by art, this fish is eternal and cannot be destroyed by time: its scales turn aside the sun's sword by their polish. Likewise, the perfect poem is a reflecting and protecting surface.

"His shield/was his humility"

The characteristic techniques of Moore's art—the verbal tactics that create a poem—can be seen as devices that in the process protect the self. The accumulation of observed detail leading to ethical generalization, the profusion of direct quotation, the self-effacing role of the speaker, the famous reticence, a desire to present without interpretation that is frequently exaggerated to the point of a blurring or confusion of point of view, the irony and wit, the subtle systems of prosody, the choice of subject and theme, even the procedure of revision and edition, all work towards this end. Yet the poems themselves have also functioned to define this procedure even as they enact it: as many of her commentators have pointed out, themes of defense, of "armor," dominate her poetry throughout her career. What is, I think, ultimately responsible for the complexity of her poetry is its stance of not talking about what it is talking about, talking about what it is not talking about: a provocative, delightful, infuriating irony that plays off itself with a dazzling shimmer.

"His Shield," which first appeared in book form in the 1951 *Collected Poems*, exemplifies many of the techniques that I have listed. It begins by describing a series of animals, recognizable as subjects for a Moore poem if only because they are unusual topics for traditional verse: porcupine, echidna, echinoderm, and hedgehog. Moore is well-known for her special bestiary, about which Donald Hall writes with insight:

> The creatures in Miss Moore's animal kingdom have qualities she would find agreeable in human beings. It is a kingdom where only brave, restrained, and self-sufficient animals are admitted. They go about their business with an efficiency that Miss Moore finds admirable. In later poems the animals are often armored with scales or quills or some other means of self-protection. They are equipped to take care of themselves in a world that seems increasingly dangerous.[33]

Not only are these particular animals "battle-dressed," but the verse itself bristles with verbal play that calls attention to the words' sharp edges.

> The pin-swin or spine-swine
> (the edgehog miscalled hedgehog) with all his edges out,
> echidna and echinoderm in distressed-
> pin-cushion thorn-fur coats, the spiny pig or porcupine,
> the rhino with horned snout—
> everything is battle-dressed.

The stanza moves from beast to beast, sound and theme in associative harmony: pins and pigs, spines and swine, horns and thorns, hedges and edges, pines and rhinos, all rhyming and twining to create a hard-outlined stanza that defines with rigid precision these armored creatures. Moore is concerned with surfaces, with the relation of dress to distress, so that only those qualities of these animals that have to do with protective covering are noticed and yoked in these opening lines.

But pig-fur (a porcupine is after all a spined swine) is contrasted in the second stanza to salamander-skin, a different mode of protection.

> Pig-fur won't do, I'll wrap
> myself in salamander-skin like Presbyter John.
> A lizard in the midst of flames, a firebrand
> that is life, asbestos-eyed asbestos eared, with tattooed nap
> and permanent pig on
> the instep; he can withstand
>
> fire and won't drown . . .

Presbyter John was a legendary Christian leader in Asia or Africa believed to wear a garment of salamander skin. Salamanders were believed to be impervious to fire; asbestos was believed to be made of salamander skin. From the association of these ideas, Moore begins to create the image of a figure moving gracefully through existence, not standing to confront but eluding attack as it goes. Whom is she describing? Her grammar makes this unclear. She begins by announcing that, for her, pig-fur, as described in the first stanza, won't do. She would prefer salamander-skin and therefore compares herself to Presbyter John. Yet the remainder of stanza and poem are devoted to John as lizard, salamander as John. We can only assume that his pattern reveals her principles. In typical fashion, she has introduced herself into the poem in the role of conversationalist.

The third stanza continues the description of Presbyter John's impenetrability, with the fluid, run-on form that links stanzas for the remainder of the poem in strong contrast to the original tight and contained stanzaic unit.

> . . . In his
> unconquerable country of unpompous gusto,
> gold was so common none considered it; greed
> and flattery were unknown. Though rubies large as tennis
> balls conjoined in streams so
> that the mountain seemed to bleed,
>
> the inextinguishable
> salamander styled himself but presbyter . . .

The fact that ethical matters are at issue in this discussion of porcupines and salamanders begins to be revealed by the inclusion of concepts such as "greed" and "flattery" into the vocabulary. To this point, as is customary in Moore's poetry, the vocabulary, the focus, has been on objects, not ideas. But for all her genuine interest in physical detail, she is a moralist at heart, and objects are always agents in a universe that is ethical and pedagogical.

The fabulous land of Presbyter John is at once innocent and opulent (itself a model garden), but even in that setting, John is special in his modesty and lack of pretentiousness. His gracious but nonostentatious salamander skin is contrasted against the rubies large as tennis balls; in the next stanza, his linen coat against the sable worn by his retinue.

Although he is unquestionably the leader of all this magnificence, he styles himself "but presbyter"—elder.

> . . . His shield
> was his humility. In Carpasian
> linen coat, flanked by his household lion cubs and sable
> retinue, he revealed
> a formula safer than
>
> an armorer's: the power of relinquishing
> what one would keep; that is freedom. Become dinosaur-
> skulled, quilled or salamander-wooled, more ironshod
> and javelin-dressed than a hedgehog battalion of steel, but be
> dull. Don't be envied or
> armed with a measuring rod.

By the final lines of the poem, the instructionary nature of its material is clear-cut. Presbyter John's actions reveal a formula for living; and in its own right revealing is the value of that formula in Moore's eyes: "safer." The poem concludes with a series of maxims, as do many of her poems. She prefers to express truth in the form of generalizations that are impersonal and global; in that way, they appear to exist independent of their speaker. One is "the power of relinquishing / what one would keep; that is freedom." Another is "be / dull. Don't be envied or / armed with a measuring rod." The most effective shield is neither quill nor spine, nor the armor of the skin, but the psychological protection that "humility" affords. Giving up what one wants before others want it from you (envy) or before you judge others with it (armed with a measuring rod) is "freedom." Freedom from what? From attack. Another, better kind of armor. The entire poem has been leading up to these observations, yet they are not entirely appropriate. As Donald Hall points out: "Humility, when you think about it, is a shield for rather curious reasons . . . After all, if one can do something well, what is the point of pretending that one can't? . . . Humility is a shield because it seeks to disarm. If you get there first with your own self-criticism you effectively take the wind from the sails of subsequent critics. This is pretty good armor, but it is questionable humility."[34] In other words, the truisms that conclude the poem, toward which the structure has been ostensibly building, seem less a description of Presbyter John's situation than of Marianne Moore's; the salamander-skin a metaphor for her shield, not his. As Hall observes: "It would be an armor necessary only to those who want, more than anything, to be best. Contrived humility can only bespeak a soul not very humble."[35]

The final stanza also contains a return, in thought and style, to the first, so that structurally the poem seems rounded off and closed. A series of animal armors are proposed as possible physical stances with wittily juxtaposed images—"Become dinosaur- / skulled, quilled or salamander-wooled." Yet the list concludes with the advice to "be / dull." A physical dullness would make all that compiled armor ineffective; a psychological dullness might look like humility but is in fact its opposite. Is Moore being ironic here, with an irony directed against her own need for defenses? Or at others for believing her advice, her talk of humility and dullness? Or both at the same time? Here, as with many lines that occur in the overt precision of Moore's vocabulary and thought, the effect is that of confusion, and the confusion is that of tone.

"His Shield" is a skillfully wrought poem with a surface of reflected edges that is admirable to see and experience. I would suggest that its seeming inconsistencies are as careful as its rhymes; that the ironic and enigmatic tone with which it concludes is what gives it its lasting power—a hint of depths that are, however, never actually visible. Remaining at all times armored by her own words, Moore never need expose herself.

"whose scales turn aside the sun's sword by their polish"

"His Shield" illustrates some of Moore's techniques as they form the pattern that is the poem. These devices occur throughout the years, although changes in emphasis may come and go.

Her ostensible subject matter, for example, is not always the animal kingdom; for not only are the animals persistent objects of appreciation in her work but they exemplify the function of the object as subject in most of her poems. The immediate and initial focus on the object is of course central to the early modern aesthetic. It locates the poem in the sensual world, the world of immediate experience. For Moore, as for many of her contemporaries, it is a kite with a tail to which many other things can be tied: impressions, ideas, philosophies. But her reticence about claiming responsibility for these additions is especially characteristic of Moore. Her earlier work, initially published during the twenties and thirties in several small volumes and collected in 1935 as *Selected Poems,* is still the material most anthologized and most well-known. Many of these poems begin with direct observation, such as "The Monkeys":

> winked too much and were afraid of snakes. The zebras,
> supreme in
> their abnormality; the elephants with their fog-colored skin
> and strictly practical appendages
> were there, the small cats . . .

Yet even in these instances, judgments (such as those of supremacy and abnormality) get attached to the objects. Pure "objectivity" is nearly impossible on the part of any observer who is also human.

More frequently, the first stanza of a Moore poem is immediately interpretative.

> "No water so still as the
> dead fountains of Versailles." No swan,
> with swart blind look askance
> and gondoliering legs, so fine
> as the chintz china one with fawn-
> brown eyes and toothed gold
> collar on to show whose bird it was.
> ("No Swan So Fine")

> I have a friend who would give a price for those long fingers all
> of one length—
> those hideous bird's claws, for that exotic asp and mongoose—
> products of the country in which everything is hard work, the
> country of the grass-getter,
> the torch-bearer, the dog-servant, the messenger-bearer, the
> holy man.
> ("Snakes, Mongooses, Snake Charmers, and the Like")

> Dürer would have seen a reason for living
> in a town like this, with eight stranded whales
> to look at; with the sweet sea air coming into your house

on a fine day, from water etched
with waves as formal as the scales
on a fish.
("The Steeple-Jack," revised version)

"No Swan So Fine," with its attitudes towards art and nature reminiscent of "An Egyptian Pulled Glass Bottle in the Shape of a Fish," begins with a quotation, identified by her notes as being the words of Percy Phillip.[36] Moore is well-known for the inclusion of quotations, frequently from obscure sources, into the body of her poems and has explained them this way: "I've always felt that if a thing has been said in the *best* way, how can you say it better?"[37] Perhaps, except that the new content into which she inserts it might well be seen as a "better" way. Irony? In any case, in the poetry, the quotations also function, as do the outside opinions with which the other two poems begin, and the maxims with which most of her poems end, to provide attitudes and pass judgments for which she is not personally responsible. As Randall Jarrell remarks: "Quotation is armour and ambiguity and irony all at once."[38] The connection between the painter Dürer and the New England town, as that between the friend and the snakes, is an essential theme in the poem. Both will subsequently point to the relation between the natural world and human use of it: "a sea the purple of the peacock's neck is / paled to greenish azure as Dürer changed / the pine green of the Tyrol to peacock blue and guinea grey"; "he gazes as if incapable of looking at anything with a view to / analysis." Often it is another human, like Presbyter John, who is observed in relation to the natural kingdom in this, one of Moore's favorite poetic structures. So that when she concludes the poem with a platitude or two—"The king is dead" ("No Swan So Fine"); "It could not be dangerous to be living / in a town like this" ("The Steeple-Jack"); "The passion for setting people right is itself an afflictive disease. / Distaste which takes no credit to itself is best" ("Snakes, Mongooses . . .")—they seem to be accounted for by sources other than herself.

In later poems, such as "What Are Years?" (1941)—which, in 1965, she calls her "best done, best written"[39]—it is perhaps a sense of self-confidence that prompts her to omit the objective correlatives. The result is a pure and overt moralizing that seems pompous: "What is our innocence, / what is our guilt? All are / naked, none is safe. And whence / is courage." When the poem concludes, "This is morality, /

this is eternity," the reader may feel that nothing in the poem has proved it; she or he may not appreciate being offered truth in so dogmatic a fashion. The mediated vision of the more characteristic Moore poem may be protecting and controlling the pure moralist, who, especially as a woman, may seem an offensive figure. The verbal techniques that so successfully disguise and protect the poet herself are also responsible for a complexity missing in a poem like "What Are Years?"

In much later poems, the occasional format that is an excuse for her best poems becomes in itself a *raison d'être*. "Rescue with Yul Brynner," "Baseball and Writing," or "Carnegie Hall: Rescued" seem almost like parodies of herself, with Ogden Nash-esque rhymes ("Assign Yogi Berra to Cape Canaveral; / he could handle any missile") and wordplay for its own sake ("Yul log for the Christmas-fire tale-spinner— / of fairy tales that can come true: Yul Brynner"). Lacking the implicit urgency of poems in which an affectation of lightness and play is one more protective device, they accomplish little.

In its finished state, a poem by Marianne Moore confronts the reader like a glittery gem (not an iceberg tip, ocean, or pool): it forbids access to anything other than itself, a self of surfaces. She was continually polishing these surfaces; for her, revision usually meant compressing, condensing. "My own revisions are usually the result of impatience with unkempt diction and lapses in logic; together with an awareness that for most defects, to delete is the instantaneous cure."[40] She also says, in her poem "To a Snail": "Contractility is a virtue / as modesty is a virtue." Effacing is preferable to facing, especially if one is unsure whether the armor is perfect.

The final version of "Poetry," a poem that began in *Poems* (1921) as thirty lines, became thirteen lines in *Observations* (1921), then thirty-eight lines in the *Selected Poems* of 1935 and the *Collected Poems* of 1951, is in the *Complete Poems* of 1967 four lines long.

> I, too, dislike it.
> Reading it, however, with a perfect contempt for it, one discovers in
> it, after all, a place for the genuine.

The irony in this final version is so thick that it bristles. The speaker is, after all, a poet, and her means of making this statement is a poem. So the first line is if nothing else challenging. The result of the second sentence is to offer highest praise: if, in this contemptible art, poetry, there is still a place for the genuine, that genuine in that poem must be rare stuff indeed. Still, one asks when the poem is over: What is she doing with this "perfect contempt" in the first place? Especially since I am woefully bereft of that quality as I read her poem! Is she so superior? Or is she so humble? Or is she laughing at herself for being a poet? Or at me for believing her when she says she dislikes it? Or at me for not knowing I should dislike it? As a piece of rhetoric, the poem is also perfect, in its precision of vocabulary and placement, the movement from "I" to "too" to "dislike" to "reading" to "however" to "perfect contempt" to "discovers" to "after all" to "place" to "genuine" revealing argument and counterargument, process and conclusion, with an economy that is both dazzling and impenetrable.

The longest version begins with the shorter one quoted, plus a comment: "there are things that are important beyond all this fiddle." The remainder of the poem expands the idea. It contains a definition of poets as "literalists of the imagination" (a quotation from William Butler Yeats) and a definition of poems as "imaginary gardens with real toads in them" (a quotation from herself, from the earliest version of the poem!). It includes as well examples of some real toads, "Hands that can grasp, eyes / that can dilate, hair that can rise / if it must," and some discussion of what can turn such facts into poor verse: "When they become so derivative as to become unintelligible."

The longer versions of "Poetry" possess neither "unkempt diction" nor "lapses in logic." If anything, they are too explicit in their explanation of the opening mystery. "Excess is the common substitute for energy," writes Moore, and "Feeling at its deepest—as we all have reason to know—tends to be inarticulate. If it does manage to be articulate, it is likely to seem overcondensed, so that the author is resisted as being enigmatic or disobliging or arrogant."[41] One reason for compression might very well have been that she felt the long versions to be too excessive. But I suspect yet another. A series of examples follows the remark "we / do not admire what / we cannot understand." These are bats, elephants, a wild horse, a tireless wolf, an immovable critic, the baseball fan, the statistician—all subjects of her own poetry. (Who is the "we," one wonders, in the light of the remark on feeling and poetry just quoted? Good readers or poor readers? Which is she?) The poem continues to observe that although these phenomena are important, they have been "dragged into prominence by half-poets." The result has not been poetry. True poets must be "above / innocence and triviality" in presenting such material, and in this way present the genuine (the pulled glass fish bottle, for example). The longer version is characteristically ambivalent about her status as true poet or half poet, but she may have found the inclusion at all of herself as poet to be too daring. In the short version, she overtly functions as reader, not writer, in the action of the poem. The subtlety of the short version is based upon our knowledge that she is nevertheless the author of the poem and we are readers, but all this is covertly expressed and therefore not liable to attack. The poem is well-described by another of her poems: "compressed; firmed by the thrust of the blast / till compact, like a bulwark against fate" ("Like a Bulwark").

Critics of Moore's work have not failed to notice her propensity for armored animals; her interest, throughout her career, in matters of danger and defense.

> A good deal of her poetry is specifically (and changingly) about armour, weapons, protection, places to hide; and she is not only conscious that this is so, but after a while writes poems about the fact that it is so. As she says, "armour seems extra," but it isn't; and when she writes about "another armoured animal," about another "thing made graceful by adversities, conversities," she does so with the sigh of someone who has come home. She asks whether a woman's looks are weapons or scalpels; comments, looking out on a quiet town: "It could scarcely be dangerous to be living / in a town like this"; says about a man's nonchalance: "his by- / play was more terrible in its effectiveness / than the fiercest frontal attack. / The staff, the bag, the feigned inconsequence / of manner, best bespeak that weapon, self-protectiveness." *That weapon, self-protectiveness!* The poet knows that morals are not "the memory of success that no longer succeeds," but a part of survival."[42]

Poems that defend the self in their process and that are about the process of self-defense are finally curious kinds of revelations. Ultimately, albeit inconclusively, the poem's objective correlative, be it pangolin, paper nautilus, or wood-weasel, hints at the presence of the poet herself. You may not be able to pin her down (you should not), but she is there.

"The Wood-Weasel" briefly epitomizes this kind of "revelation." It begins by conversationally describing its subject, who "emerges daintily, the skunk– / don't laugh–in sylvan black and white chipmunk / regalia." Once again the focus will be on armor: "The inky thing / adaptively whited with glistening / goat fur. . . ." Word-fun will reflect, connect to theme, as black protection is played against white protection with rhyme and chime: "In his / ermined well-cuttlefish-inked wool, he is / determination's totem. Out- / lawed?" Through inclusion of associated objects in the description, through inclusion as the description progresses of a moral vocabulary ("Determination's totem"), the poet hints at the wood-weasel's status as exemplar.

After depicting him, she goes on to explain how his brand of armor works.

> He is his own protection from the moth,
>
> noble little warrior. That
> otter-skin on it, the living polecat,
> smothers anything that stings.

As we have come to expect, his technique is not aggressive but self-protective, a form of passivity.

> . . . Well,
> this same weasel's playful and his weasel
> associates are too. Only
> wood-weasels shall associate with me.

With grace and a certain haze, Moore appears at the poem's conclusion. The logical progression of the last lines goes like this: wood-weasels are playful; wood-weasel associates are playful; therefore, if only wood-weasels shall associate with me, I am a wood-weasel associate, and I am playful. I am a weasel, perhaps, since "weasel associates" might mean either associates who are weasels or associates of weasels. But weasels, we know from the rest of the poem, are more than purely playful: they are playful in their manner of self-protection. As are the poem's last lines, spoken by a person who authoritatively if playfully claims wood-weasels as her sole companions. Ironic, surely, since as a person and not a weasel she is probably not proposing to retire to the forests. Probably she is proposing the wood-weasel as a model for living, a model that attracts her, perhaps because it reflects her own style of playful self-protection. Perhaps she has chosen to write about the wood-weasel in the first place because he is like her, rather than because she is like him. Perhaps. There is no way of ever answering these questions, so she is safe, having effectively smothered with her words anything that might sting.

Her long poem "Marriage" may be on the subject of women, but it is not about women who are poets, and it is not about Marianne Moore. One small poem is, however, directly about herself, yet at the same time predictably mysterious and maddening in its revelations. Possessing that filtered knowledge of Moore as woman poet that her other poems half reveal helps in reading it.

O to Be a Dragon

If I, like Solomon, . . .
could have my wish—

my wish . . . O to be a dragon,
a symbol of the power of Heaven—of silkworm
size or immense; at times invisible.
Felicitous phenomenon!

The opening "if" is a typical disclaimer, as is the fabulous status of the dragon; but the urgency of the wish is still there: the long, strong "O." What better defense than pure invisibility; what clearer equation than that between size and control over it? The mythical dragon, Moore has pointed out, as primary symbol of the Tao, is "symbol of the power of heaven," not its own;[43] thus the seat of power is thrice-removed from the poet. This dragon is associated with "a 'oneness' that is tireless; whereas egotism, synonymous with ignorance in Buddhist thinking, is tedious." For Moore a perfect symbol for her desires, to possess power without personal responsibility for having it. Nevertheless, the desire for power is heartfelt; it is the feeling for which this poem is needed as articulation. When one is not invisible, one might be immense, the largest creature that the human imagination has created. The phenomenon is felicitous and so is the form: apt. An understatement, an ironic statement, a well-defended statement, but a revelation nonetheless.

Marianne Moore would wish to be a dragon, a creature that is not—powerful over all, but imaginary. Neither, in her world, is the woman poet someone possible to be. The woman poet cancels herself out in self-contradiction, as Moore knows and reveals. She admires herself so much that she is afraid to show it; she is so ashamed of herself that she is afraid to show it. The different facets of her being cannot ever appear onstage together, and the best defense of all is not to appear to be onstage. In the protective skin of wood-weasel or salamander one might take a part. But if one removed that armor for the curtain call, there might be no one inside. Denying the self can understandably cause one to question its existence.

Marianne Moore did not exaggerate her sense of danger. In her life and in her art, she trod delicately, purposefully, skillfully through enemy lines, deflecting attack by eluding it, by denying it, by never appearing to be at battle and thus gaining a victory that may have been qualified by the very methods used to gain it but which was nevertheless a prize that few before her had won.

NOTES

1. Vassar opened in 1865, Smith and Wellesley in 1875, the "Harvard Annex" (Radcliffe) in 1879, and Bryn Mawr in 1885. Mt. Holyoke, opened as a seminary in 1837, received collegiate status in 1893.
2. F. S. Flint, "Imagism," *Poetry* 1, no. 6 (March 1913): 199.
3. Ezra Pound, "A Few Don'ts by an Imagist," *Poetry* 1, no. 6 (March 1913): 200–201.
4. Suzanne Juhasz, *Metaphor and the Poetry of Williams, Pound, and Stevens* (Lewisburg, Pennsylvania: Bucknell University Press, 1974), p. 20.
5. T. S. Eliot, "Hamlet and His Problems," *Selected Essays* (New York: Harcourt, Brace & Co., 1950), p. 125.
6. Louis Zukofsky, *An Objectivist's Anthology*, quoted in Bernard Engel, *Marianne Moore* (New York: Twayne, 1964), p. 18.
7. Donald Hall, "The Art of Poetry: Marianne Moore," *Writers at Work: The Paris Review Interviews*, Second Series (New York: Viking Press, 1963), p. 63.
8. Marianne Moore, "A Burning Desire to Be Explicit," *Tell Me, Tell Me* (New York: Viking Press, 1966), p. 5.
9. *The Complete Poems of Marianne Moore* (New York: Viking Press, 1967), p. 62. All references to Moore's poetry are to this volume unless otherwise stated.
10. Marianne Moore, "If I Were Sixteen Today," *A Marianne Moore Reader* (New York: Viking Press, 1961), p. 196.
11. T. S. Eliot, Introduction to *Selected Poems by Marianne Moore* (London: Faber and Faber, 1935), p. 6.
12. William Carlos Williams, "Marianne Moore," *Selected Essays* (New York: New Directions, 1969), p. 128.
13. Kenneth Burke, "Motives and Motifs in the Poetry of Marianne

Moore," in Charles Tomlinson, ed., *Marianne Moore: A Collection of Critical Essays* (Englewood Cliffs, New Jersey: Prentice-Hall, 1969), p. 96.

14. Donald Hall, *Marianne Moore: The Cage and the Animal* (New York: Pegasus, 1970).
15. William Carlos Williams, *Autobiography* (New York: New Directions, 1951), p. 146.
16. William Wasserman, "Irregular Symmetry: Marianne Moore's *Dial*," in Tambimuttu, ed., *"Festschrift" for Marianne Moore's Seventy-Seventh Birthday* (New York: Tambimuttu and Mass, 1964), p. 33.
17. Margueritte Young, "An Afternoon with Marianne Moore," in Tambimuttu, ed., *"Festschrift" for Marianne Moore's Seventy-Seventh Birthday,* p. 64.
18. Malcolm Cowley, "Speech Delivered at the Dinner Meeting of the National Institute of Arts and Letters on the Occasion of Marianne Moore's 75th Birthday, November 1962," in Tambimuttu, ed., *"Festschrift" for Marianne Moore's Seventy-Seventh Birthday,* p. 120.
19. Robert Penn Warren, "Jingle: In Tribute to a Great Poem by Marianne Moore," in Tambimuttu, ed., *"Festschrift" for Marianne Moore's Seventy-Seventh Birthday,* p. 103.
20. Donald Hall, "An Interview with Marianne Moore," *McCall's* 92 (December 1965): 183.
21. Ibid., p. 182.
22. Hall, *Writers at Work: The Paris Review Interviews,* p. 70.
23. Roy Harvey Pearce, *The Continuity of American Poetry* (Princeton: Princeton University Press, 1961), p. 366.
24. Tomlinson, ed., *Marianne Moore: A Collection of Critical Essays,* p. 12.
25. Ibid., p. 122.
26. Williams, *Selected Essays,* p. 123.
27. Jean Garrigue, "Notes Towards a Resemblance: Emily Dickinson, Marianne Moore," in Tambimuttu, ed., *"Festschrift" for Marianne Moore's Seventy-Seventh Birthday,* p. 52.
28. Pearce, *The Continuity of American Poetry,* p. 372.
29. Henry Gifford, "Two Philologists," in Tomlinson, ed., *Marianne Moore: A Collection of Critical Essays,* p. 172.
30. Ibid., p. 173.
31. Ibid., p. 176.
32. Marianne Moore, "Feeling and Precision," in *Predilections* (New York: Viking Press, 1955), p. 11.
33. Hall, *Marianne Moore: The Cage and the Animal,* p. 78.
34. Ibid., p. 127.
35. Ibid., p. 128.

36. *The New York Times Magazine*, May 10, 1931.
37. Hall, *Writers at Work: The Paris Review Interviews*, p. 73.
38. Jarrell, "Her Shield," in Tomlinson, ed., *Marianne Moore: A Collection of Critical Essays*, p. 120.
39. Hall, "An Interview with Marianne Moore," p. 190.
40. "Idiosyncracy and Technique," *A Marianne Moore Reader*, p. 170.
41. "Feeling and Precision," in *Predilections*, pp. 9, 3.
42. Jarrell, "Her Shield," in Tomlinson, ed., *Marianne Moore: A Collection of Critical Essays*, pp. 119–20.
43. Foreword to *A Marianne Moore Reader*, p. xiv.

4

"The Enactment of Rites": The Poetry of Denise Levertov

Feminine Poetry

By mid-century, the sex of many women poets becomes less of a well-kept professional secret. They begin to write more specifically about their own experience, which is frequently shaped by the fact of their womanhood. I call this poetry "feminine," both to call attention to the fact that feminine experience contributes more directly to the themes and the forms of these poems and also to distinquish it from the feminist poetry that will develop in the late 1960's. When these poets are political, their politics are more governmental than sexual. That is, they might find "poet" to be a political word, but not "woman." They use, to a greater or lesser degree, their feminine experience as a source for poetry because it has been their own experience but not to raise consciousness about women.

It is thanks to the efforts of the earlier generations of American women poets that they can do even *this* much. Because there is a tradition of names behind them, they need not be so fearful to reveal the fact of their sex. Societal pressures upon women artists have not lessened, but there is at least a company of resisters to join! A tradition is being created, although at this period it is not yet a self-conscious one.

Some of the women who reach poetic maturity in mid-century, poets like Adrienne Rich and Carolyn Kizer, develop into strong feminist poets. Here, however, I shall discuss Denise Levertov, Sylvia Plath, and Anne Sexton as examples of those women poets (including May Swenson, Mona Van Duyn, Shirley Kaufman, Maxine Kumin, Isabella Gardner, Vassar Miller, and others) who, as "feminine" poets, are establishing the tenets, themes, and forms of the new tradition.

Levertov, Plath, and Sexton have in common the fact that each writes from personal, feminine experience. The work of these poets represents three modes or stages in the evolution of poetry by women. Levertov's poetry derives most directly from the masculine tradition that dominates modern poetry, although both its recurrent ambivalence and frequent flashes of vibrant strength seem to me to arise out of an engagement with her feminine experience. Plath's career, tragically cut off at what is really its beginning, nevertheless shows a movement away from traditional forms and attitudes towards a more idiosyncratic poetry that is closely linked to her experiences as a woman in society. Sexton begins where the others leave off, with an involvement in her feminine experience that is often labeled "confessionalism." Yet, unlike the confessionalism of many male poets (Robert Lowell's, for example, in *Life Studies*),[1] Sexton's poetry does not plug into a larger tradition—that of being a poet whose life and consciousness is in some sense and to some degree meant to typify the consciousness of his age. No such tradition exists for the woman poet: she has never been the voice of her age (and may never want to be). Never losing its basis in her personal self and life, Sexton's voice does develop, in the direction of magic and myth, and her forms alter correspondingly until her death in 1974.

Levertov, the most established, the most famous, the oldest of the three poets, occupies a significant and transitional position in the history of poetry by women because her work contains elements of both the dominant masculine and the emerging feminine traditions. She seems to see herself as poet, not as woman poet. Over the twenty-five years of her poetic career, her work has grown in skill and refinement, but there has been little change in either her aesthetic theories or the forms in which they are rendered. Writing closely within a mainstream of modern poetry—"imagistic," "organic"—she also brings to her work a spiritual, religious element and particular kind of personalism (that of her feminine experience). Sometimes these elements work together in harmony; at other times they struggle with one another, affecting the unity of a given poem. A need to abstract and to generalize upon the greater significance of an experience (a distancing movement found in both the poetic and the spiritual traditions in which she works) is sometimes at odds with an involvement and an immediacy that arise most strongly in poems that deal with intense personal experience (in particular, the feminine and the political).

Plath is the woman poet of our century who sees the double bind inherent in trying to be both woman and poet with the coldest, most unredeeming clarity: her life and her art embody her attempts to find a solution. She never finds one. The conflict as she experiences it is between her woman's body (object, all surfaces, illusion; or else inner space, fertility, but also, in the end, illusion) and her poet's mind (vision, reality, and death). As a person who sees division, separation, within her very self, who is conscious of surfaces and interiors everywhere and of the gap between them, she sees the pulse of life as the movement towards disintegration; the stasis of death as the only integration. Her later poetry enacts symbolically the struggle between life and death that is occurring in her consciousness, in her life. Over a period of ten years, her art develops from a glittery poetry of surfaces, in which the poet, observing the external world, orders and controls it through the power of her language to dissect and reassemble, to a poetry of engagement and integration, in which the sole source of reality is her own consciousness, in which objects from the external world are meaningful only as they define that consciousness, in which the outside world has been pulled inside the mind.

Sexton comes to poetry as an adult. She becomes a poet *after* having experienced the traditional woman's roles of wife, mother, housewife; *because* she has experienced them and needs a way, a form, a voice with which to deal with the fact of being a woman. Sexton's journey from the private suffering of woman's experience to power derived from her public role, and voice as poet has been the movement of her poetry itself. The act of her poems is what brings her from the death of madness to the life of the poet; the exploration, in poetry, of her own self. Therefore, her identity as a poet is rooted in her identity as a woman. Her early poems probe for the truth through endless explorations of herself as she has been created by interpersonal relationships with mother, father, daughters. But though her poetry begins as therapy for her personal salvation, because poetry is a public act, it reaches out to others. By rooting her public voice in her private experience, by creating a public persona, witch, out of her private self, witch, she is able to discuss the race in addition to herself. Her last poetry is no longer "confessional," because the talking voice, immersing itself in memory and experience, is gone; the voice chants or sings, and experience has been transformed into myth. Nevertheless, the poems still refuse to generalize, to abstract; they rather present a world of visionary truth-saying.

"We have the words in our pockets"

Denise Levertov has explicitly and implicitly, in verse and in prose, acknowledged her indebtedness to that early generation of modern poets whom she has called "the old great ones": William Carlos Williams, Ezra Pound, H. D.

> This is the year the old ones,
> the old great ones
> leave us alone on the road.
>
> The road leads to the sea.
> We have the words in our pockets,
> obscure directions . . .
>
> They have told us
> the road leads to the sea,
> and given
>
> the language into our hands.
>
> ("September 1961")[2]

Since her association in the fifties with the Black Mountain poets (Charles Olson, Robert Creeley, and others, all heirs of Williams), she has grown to poetic maturity within a mainstream of American poetry. Like Williams, she uses language to render the rhythms of an experience and believes in the richness and significance of the everyday, the quotidian. The poet's job, as she describes it in "Some Notes on Organic Form,"[3] is to discover and reveal the form that preexists in all things. Experience, which for her can be intellectual, emotional, and sensory, is the content of her poetry; artistic form is a revelation of content. Sensitive and adept at writing this kind of "organic" poetry, she is, however, not initiating any new aesthetic theory as her gift to poetry. One reason why she has become one of the best-known of contemporary poets, I think, is that she is so solidly within the masculine tradition of her masters and associates. Nevertheless, she is far from being a "female Williams." There are other elements and attributes to her poetry that make it distinctly her own.

From her Russian Jewish ancestry (at least in part), she brings a concern with the spiritual, the ritual, the religious element of living that goes far beyond Williams's sensuality. Characteristically, she finds the spiritual to be an intensification and a clarification of the everyday event: "I don't want to escape, only to see / the enactment of rites," she remarks in an early poem ("The Room").[4] Her poems themselves are rites, moving around an experience and with the insight of words granting it significance, even holiness. The clarification that is achieved comes from the poet's ability to see with the waking mind what its unconscious counterpart has always known in dreams. Levertov's poetry constantly explores the relation between the inner world of dream and the outer world of action precisely because this dynamic is the very source of poetry itself:

> . . . What gate
> opens, dim there in the mind's
> field, river mists of the sky
> veiling its guardian?
> ("Under a Blue Star")[5]

Levertov's work differs from Williams's in another way: because she is a woman, the experience that her poems require for their existence is feminine experience. The dominant qualities of those experiences of nature, art, people, and politics that make up her poems are their personal and private nature and their circumscribed boundaries. Such qualities have come to be associated with women's experience, so on that level Levertov's poetry seems very feminine. Even when her poetry becomes more public in its involvement with political issues, such as the Vietnam war, it continues to explore these problems in relation to everyday and private life.

> The disasters numb within us
> caught in the chest, rolling
> in the brain like pebbles. The feeling
> resembles lumps of raw dough

weighing down a child's stomach on baking day.
("Life at War," *The Sorrow Dance*)[6]

The moment of intense experience remains the unit of her poetic discourse.

On the other hand, the strong influence of the masculine tradition often causes her to step away from the experience that her poem has revealed, to abstract and generalize upon its greater significance, following Williams's dictum: "in the particular to discover the universal."[7] She is consistently concerned with the meaning of an event, and meaning is usually a concept: "the authentic," "joy," "the devil," "revolution." The way to discover meaning is to experience it—"Grief in the morning, washed away / in coffee, crumbled to a dozen errands between / busy fingers" ("A Lamentation")[8]—but the experience, and the poem, is somehow incomplete for her unless she takes that generalizing and abstracting step. In addition, she is characteristically an observer, participating through sympathy or even empathy in the world around her but not through direct involvement; frequently, she as poet acts through the actions of others.

Leather Jacket

She turns, eager—
hand going out to touch
his arm. But touches
a cold thick sleeve.
1970

(*Footprints*)

Because her work contains these elements of both the dominant masculine and the emerging feminine traditions, Levertov occupies a position in the history of modern poetry that is transitional and significant. This duality frequently results not in an androgyny but in an ambiguity in individual poems, one reason why I personally find her poetry to be skillful and beautiful but often, in the end, unsatisfying. (My students often complain that her poetry is "cold," disengaged. They admire what they call her "sanity" or "healthiness"—as contrasted to the confusions and anxieties of Plath or Sexton—but her poetry often fails to involve them in its world.)

"Marvelous Truth, confront us / at every turn"

In her attempts to reveal experience in art, it is essential for Levertov that she communicate not only its sensory elements but also its significance or meaning. Knowledge of that significance comes from the poet's artistry, her skill at creating a language that will release all aspects of an experience; it comes, as well, from attuning herself to an inner source of truth, the life of the unconscious, of dreams. The knowledge, finally, can come out of a personal involvement or participation in an experience that is so strong that any generalizations about it become, in a sense, unnecessary.

Experience of nature, art, people; of love, politics, friendship; of the worlds of dream and myth—these have been the material of Levertov's poetry, collected in seven major American volumes, over the last fifteen years, since her leaving England and attaining maturity as an American poet. Historical progression is largely absent from her work. The poems continue to concern themselves with similar areas of experience, with only the political element increasing in importance; she refines and polishes her techniques, but they, too, show little change. This is why I am discussing her poetry thematically and structurally, rather than chronologically.

"There is a poetry that in thought and in feeling and in perception seeks the forms peculiar to these experiences," she writes.[9] In "Some Notes on Organic Form," she talks about the poet's "form sense," "the sense the poet's ear has of some rhythmic norm peculiar to a particular poem, from which the individual lines depart and to which they return."[10] I call this process the poet's way of "tracing" an experience with words to make a poem. Williams does it, as in "Poem":[11]

> As the cat
> climbed over
> the top of
>
> the jamcloset
> first the right
> forefoot
>
> carefully
> then the hind
> stepped down

into the pit of
the empty
flowerpot

Levertov does it, too, as in a poem like "Exchange," in which her words create both a sensory perception of the sight and sound of sea gulls and an intellectual perception of the significance of their being inland, on her territory.

Exchange

Sea gulls inland.
Come for a change of diet,
a breath of
earth-air.

I smell the
green, dank, amber, soft
undersides of an old pier in their cries.
(*Footprints*)

There is an exchange in the fact that the gulls can have a breath of "earth-air," while the poet can smell sea places, "the / green, dank, amber, soft / undersides of an old pier." The exchange occurring between poet and gulls is reflected in a dimension of the poet's experience of the gulls; the sensation evoked in her by their sound is that of smell. This is synesthesia—the conflation, or exchange, of sensory qualities. The experience as a whole, while brief and seemingly simple, turns out to be equally topsy-turvy, unsettling, and rich. Its significance for the poet lies precisely in the fact that something so *strange* and wonderful can happen quite suddenly in an everyday moment. The poetic language itself, which begins with a matter-of-fact, spare description of the components of the situation, then pauses with an elaboration of the sensation of the gulls' cries ("green, dank, amber, soft"). is meant to render this experience in language, as is, also, the rhythm of the words, their cadence, the very way in which each line of the poem forms and breaks—like waves, like wings.

In poems of this sort, the poet operates within her or his own medium of language very much as does the painter with brush and paint: looking, imitating—not copying, but translating. Since the experience is always composed of both the external event and the artist's response to that event, the medium must express both. The artist projects her or his response out onto the physical scene and "paints" them both together, as Levertov does in "Exchange."

To match form to experience is an activity as old as art: what have changed historically are ideas about what form is, what experience is, what forms are suitable to what experiences and in what ways. Women poets as well as men poets can make and have made and do make art in which form is a revelation of content—*i.e.*, "organic" art. There appears to be no sex difference here. Sex differences, or preferences, are rather involved with the old questions: What kinds of experiences? What kinds of forms? It is this looking out at an experience, this objectifying, abstracting, and generalizing of one's subjective experience, that has been typical of the most personal of male poets, like Williams; and this is something that many women have found alien, or, in the present tense of feminist poetry, destructive, oppressive. But I am leaping ahead of myself. All that I want to say now is that when Levertov operates in this fashion, as in "Exchange" and in most of her poems, she is following directly in the masculine tradition of "imaginative voyeurism" that Williams helped to create.

Writing about the influence of Williams upon her poetry, Levertov notes that she took from him nothing of the profound mythic element of works like *Paterson*, "but rather the sharp eye for the material world and the keen ear for the vernacular which characterize his earlier and shorter poems."[12] Yet in all of her definitions of poetry and in a great many of her poems, the mythic element is very much present. "The poet—when he is writing—is a priest; the poem is a temple; epiphanies and communion take place within it. . . . Writing the poem is the poet's means of summoning the divine; the reader's may be through reading the poem, or through what the experience of the poem leads to."[13] "A religious devotion to the truth, to the splendor of the authentic, involves the writer in a process rewarding in itself; but when that devotion brings us to undreamed abysses and we find ourselves sailing slowly over them and landing on the other side—that's ecstasy."[14] Levertov's concern as a poet is not only with events but with their transcendent underskirts, or overskirts—with, in other words, the meaning of an experience. An experience without meaning is not proper subject matter for a poem; but then, conversely, all experience *must* have meaning: such is the cornerstone of her system of beliefs. All experience relates in some way to the truth, the authentic. But how?

How does the poet know? One way is to uncover with language the form inherent in all experience, no matter how chaotic or formless it might at first appear, might appear to other people, nonpoets; or to the poet before contemplating it (to contemplate means "not simply to observe, to regard , but to do these things in the presence of a god").[15] Another way is to attune oneself to one's *inner* source of truth—the life of the unconscious, the life of dream—and to connect inner knowledge with external event. She writes that in an age when the Western intellectual, along with the rest of the people, is rarely in touch with a folkloric tradition of myth and epic, "dreams may be a more frequent and . . . a more authentic source of myth in poetry than a scholarly knowledge would be."[16] A poem like "Under a Blue Star" is a description of that encounter with the inner world.

Under a Blue Star

Under a blue star, dragon of skygate . . .
Such wakenings into twilight, forebodings intermingled
with joy, beyond
hope of knowledge. The days
a web of wires, of energies vibrating
in chords and single
long notes of song; but nights
afloat on dreams, dreams
that float silent, or leave word
of blue sky-dragons, to seduce
the day's questions, drown them
in twilight before dawn. . . . What gate
opens, dim there in the mind's
field, river-mists of the sky
veiling its guardian?

(*Footprints*)

The poem opens with a quotation, its source unacknowledged, a practice common in Levertov's poetry. In "Origins of a Poem," she mentions that she keeps two notebooks, one of "brief essential texts," the other a journal that includes "meditations or ruminations" on these texts.[17] Often her poems seem to be expansions of those meditations, in which the quotations themselves are treated as objects in the world;

the meditations that they occasion are experiences. Such is the body of this poem.

After the cryptic mention of a blue star and a dragon of skygate, the poet seems to ignore these figures and comments upon the act of waking from sleep, expressing her feeling of understanding something, something both sad and happy ("forebodings intermingled / with joy") yet not intellectually comprehended. She wakes into "twilight." Why twilight? We need more of the poem to be able to answer. This first moment of the poem is the time in which night world and day world exist, briefly, concurrently. But almost immediately night is effaced by day, a day world described metaphorically as "a web of wires." It is the intellectual energy of the mind that is being equated with an electrical system producing thought and sound and even song. The day world is contrasted to the night world of dreams, a floating, silent world, unlike the busy hum of the mind at day. Yet this dream world works upon and affects the day world with its own gentle actions: leaving word (of dragons), seducing (the day's questions), drowning (those questions). The dreams replace questions rather than answer them, because two different "languages" (that of night and day) are involved. These questions are drowned in twilight—that twilight that we queried, with a daytime mind, earlier in the poem, now identified as water. Dreams replace questions drowned in twilight with word of blue sky-dragons—of fantastic, mythic beings.

Accepting the actuality of the dream world, understanding by means of the process of the poem what she had dimly felt at the moment of waking from a dream that had left her word of skygate dragons under a blue star, the poet now creates the dream landscape with the language of her poem (a combination of day language and dream language). A gate, a field, a river, a mist, a guardian (the dragon). In the final lines of the poem, she is describing the landscape of her own mind, revealed to her in dream, in which sky and water are one, in which twilight and dawn are one: these are the misted moments of half light, half worlds, where visionary knowledge is guarded by a dragon, a mythical creature who stands at the gate dividing the dream mind from the waking mind. Yet through the process of poetry itself the gate can be opened, so that this poem is a description of the moment in which the poet makes contact with that inner world that is the source of her poetry. The poem is a meditation, then a vision, understanding the significance of the quotation about a skygate dragon that had been affecting her. Even in a poem about the sources and processes of poetry itself (there are many such poems in Levertov's work), the poetic format that I described earlier remains consistent: the poem traces an experience and comes to an understanding of its significance.

Poems that describe experiences that are specifically feminine do not form the majority of Levertov's work: I have made a list of thirty poems from the seven volumes, containing hundreds of poems, that I am discussing.[18] Yet, for me at any rate, these are the poems that dominate her work. (When I first began to read Levertov in 1967, I remember that what impressed me so about her poetry, back before I was a feminist, was the combination of technical skill and a subject matter, her feminine experience, that I could "really relate to"!) In reexamining these poems, I find that their strength lies in the fact that usually the immediate, personal experience occasioning the poem is more vivid and more essential to its effectiveness than the generalizations in which it results. Such experiences are personal not only because they happen to her and not to someone or something being observed by her, but because she is the "main actor" in the event. They are, for example, less about her husband, whom she loves, than about loving her husband.

"From the Roof"[19] is a good example of a poem dominated by this kind of personal experience. It describes taking in washing from a Manhattan rooftop clothesline, an occasion that brings into focus for the poet her thoughts about the significance of her move to a new home. The move is connected to her feelings of renewed closeness towards her husband. As we have come to expect, the poem as it develops moves away from the physical experience itself to understand its intellectual meaning. That meaning is related to the elements of myth and ritual contained in the poem. For example, the crippled broom vendor from whom she had bought a broom for the new home is thought of as perhaps "one of the Hidden Ones": that is, a prophet or hidden angel,[20] and the poem is concerned with the workings of destiny and fate. Yet for me the poem's strength lies in its evocation of the washing on the clothesline and of the close emotional connection between the washing and her feelings for her husband.

In the first stanza, set on a windy evening, the poet's feelings of joy turn the clothing into flowers, animal vines, live creatures that themselves experience merriment as they gesticulate:

> This wild night, gathering the washing as if it were flowers
> animal vines twisting over the line and
> slapping my face lightly, soundless merriment
> in the gesticulations of shirtsleeves,
> I recall out of my joy a night of misery

The clothing shares in the poet's sense of being alive, even as her joy infuses the clothing with animate qualities from all realms of life. Everything is in motion: a sensuous touching and being touched; but the joy immediately recalls its absence, a night of misery, when physical closeness bred no such intimacy:

> walking in the dark and the wind over broken earth
> halfmade foundations and unfinished
> drainage trenches and the spaced-out
> circles of glaring light
> marking streets that were to be,
> walking with you but so far from you,

The couple walked in an artificial, sterile landscape, a lifeless man-made world reflecting their own emotional coldness.

The paradox of that situation (physically together, emotionally apart) has been replaced by another: now, gathering in the washing, although alone on the roof, the poet feels "so close" to her husband. The scene of roof and river view that she sees extends the evening's vitality for her, for all is personified: the season is "October's / first decision towards winter," her arms are full of linen that is "playful, rebellious," the Harborside Terminal on the Jersey shore has "green wolf-eyes" that glitter, the subway on which her husband must now be riding is bringing him towards her and their new living place:

> and now alone in October's
> first decision towards winter, so close to you—
> my arms full of playful rebellious linen, a freighter
> going down-river two blocks away, outward bound,
> the green wolf-eyes of the Harborside Terminal
> glittering on the Jersey shore,
> and a train somewhere under ground bringing you towards me
> to our new living place from which we can see

To define the quality of her experience, the poet has created a correspondence between human emotional space and physical space and objects. Life, the sense of being alive, comes from/results from an interaction between people and things: the poet is emotionally alive; so is the physical world she experiences. The contrary is also true: dead feelings both seek out and result in a dead environment, as in the walk that the poet and her husband had taken through a very different city landscape. As the poem continues, the nature of this interaction is enriched and expanded, as the poet begins to include in it a spiritual element. Continuing to look at the view before her, she observes both the Hudson River and "the hidden river"; she remembers yesterday's broom vendor who was both broom vendor and "one of the Hidden Ones": "who can say which it is we see, we see / something of both."

> a river and its traffic (the Hudson and the
> hidden river, who can say which it is we see, we see
> something of both. Or who can say
> the crippled broom-vendor yesterday, who passed
> just as we needed a new broom, was not
> one of the Hidden Ones?)

Everything has a spiritual identity: the river is neither the Hudson nor the hidden river, it is both at once, for both levels of meaning exist at all times. Sometimes we can see this, sometimes not; and poems, for Levertov, are vehicles for seeing. With her poem she sees the existence of patterns in life, always at work; designs that come from the spiritual correspondence of people with environments. It is her recognition of this design in her own life that illuminates the moment of the poem, that makes river lights and crates of fruit brilliant and a fitting part of their "new place," the setting for joy and love.

> Crates of fruit are unloading
> across the street on the cobbles,
> and a brazier flaring
> to warm the men and burn trash. He wished us
> luck when we bought the broom. But not luck
> brought us here. By design
>
> clear air and cold wind polish
> the river lights, by design
> we are to live in a new place.

The poem has moved from a sensuous experience to an awareness of the spiritual elements that complement the sensuous and expand its significance. To find a design in the varied elements of an event—flapping clothes, poet standing high on a rooftop, new home, husband moving towards her, crippled broom vendor offering new brooms that surely sweep clean—to see a pattern of fate that connects the emotional lives of one married couple to a tradition of hermetic knowledge rooted in concepts of design and destiny is once again to abstract and generalize. The spiritual interpretation of the event offers an explanation of its seeming paradoxes: the moving and not moving, the being together and apart, in a way that the purely emotive does not. It ties them to a larger tradition rooted in such paradoxes, where rivers and broom vendors are both what they seem and not what they seem: paradoxes are necessary to reveal those kinds of truths in which the unseen is what defines and makes meaningful the seen. Yet, when I remember this poem, I see Denise Levertov on the roof, with the river and its lights below her and the clean clothes thrashing in her arms, thinking of her husband with love, thinking with pleasure of their new home. That event is what drew and continues to draw me to the poem, so that I find the hidden river and the magic broom vendor to be interesting extensions of the situation but not vital to it. Levertov would, I am sure, disagree with me. Therefore, the poem is to some degree ambivalent, because the poet's intent and the poem's effect do not coincide.

Another poem that follows a pattern similar to "From the Roof" is "Matins" (*The Jacob's Ladder*), one of the clearest expressions of Levertov's ideas about poetry and meaning. The poem is initiated by an experience that we have found to be a frequent source for her poetry: the memory of a dream. This dream, happening just before waking, offers the poet shadows of the "authentic," but the nature of the authentic is imprecisely recognized.

> It thrusts up close. Exactly in dreams
> it has you off-guard, you
> recognize it before you have time.
> For a second before waking
> the alarm bell is a red conical hat, it
> takes form.

The shadow or undercurrent of this dream persists into the poet's morning activities—sitting on the toilet, brushing her hair, hearing the radiator knock, feeding breakfast to her child, and she seeks to recognize the authentic:

> The authentic, I said
> breaking the handle of my hairbrush as I
> brushed my hair in
> rhythmic strokes: That's it,
> that's joy, it's always
> a recognition, the known
> appearing fully itself, and
> more itself than one knew.
>
> (ii)

She begins to recognize that the authentic has something to do with the very rhythms of her existence, rhythms inside her that echo the knockings of the rising steam in the pipes, the new day rising as the heat rises ("knocking in the pipes / with rhythms it seizes for its own / to speak of its invention"), the rhythms of her own rituals of every day.

> Stir the holy grains, set
> the bowls on the table and
> call the child to eat.
>
> (v)

The very act of carrying out her day, of following through the "transformations of the day / in its turning, in its becoming," is what brings her closer to the recognition of the authentic, to the dream itself, the "undercurrent of dream" that "runs through us / faster than thought / towards recognition." As well as recognizing the movement of the authentic as a rhythmical rising, she understands that the authentic is itself like an egg:

> the real, the new-laid
> egg whose speckled shell
> the poet fondles and must break
> if he will be nourished.
>
> (iii)

The real (the idea of the authentic neatly combines both truth and reality) is, in other words, something vital that the poet must physically experience, eat, before she can make a poem. Once again this poem about toilets, toothpaste, and cereal is a poem about poetry itself.

At last, in stanza vii, the poet, who has just followed her child down the stairs to give him the glasses he had forgotten as he left for school, to "save / his clear sight," encounters there at the street door in the cold air her dream. (One vision deserves another!) The authentic rolls like the ball, the egg that it is, just out of reach, down a green slope and into the sea. It is now an iron ball, and the poet asks the little horse who is also present how to follow the iron ball to the country beneath the waves:

> to the place where I must kill you and you step out
> of your bones and flystrewn meat
> tall, smiling, renewed,
> formed in your own likeness.
>
> (vi)

Levertov has provided a gloss, in "The Sense of Pilgrimage," for this reference to horse and iron ball:

> In section vi of these meditations on the idea of "the authentic," the Irish tale of Conn-Edda is summarized, as it were, and in section vii is referred to, though the name of Conn-Edda is never mentioned. It happened this way. One day when I had written most of the rest of the poem but not finished it, I read the story as recounted by Heinrich Zimmer in *The King and the Corpse*; and that night I dreamed the story with myself as Conn-Edda—dreamt it in the first person. I therefore believed myself justified in incorporating my dream-experience into the poem without a note, feeling that I had *made it my own.*[21]

Levertov's point is well taken, to the extent that the reader does not have to know the story to understand its significance in this poem. The reader can see that the poem has moved from an external, everyday, physical experience into an internal, mythic, spiritual one; has in fact opened the gate described in "Under a Blue Star" and united those two realms of experience that are usually divided. The details of the particular myth that has been evoked are interesting but not essential, even as knowledge of the Zohar complements the understanding of hidden rivers in "From the Roof" but is not essential to it.

In the final section, the poet, in summarizing the movement of her poem, shows what she has learned about the authentic:

> Marvelous Truth, confront us
> at every turn,
> in every guise, iron ball,
> egg, dark horse, shadow,
> cloud
> of breath on the air,
>
> (vii)

It is important that one can encounter truth and reality—the authentic—in everyday life, in "crowded hearts," "steaming bathrooms, kitchens full of / things to be done, the / ordinary streets," but it is equally important that in order to do so one must also be sensitive to the other side of experience, to the dreams and visions that the mind also knows, and be able to relate the two. Only in this way, the poem has taught her, can a person know "terrible joy." As we have come to expect in a Levertov poem, the movement of "Matins" is built upon a particular event or sequence of events: in this instance, feminine experience, for that morning world whose rhythms the poet encounters and enacts is a woman's world. Characteristically, she uses these experiences for the purpose of reaching the greatest of generalities, "Marvelous Truth" itself.

"Into your own depths as into a poem"

When Kenneth Rexroth writes that Levertov has "a very special sensibility and completely feminine insight,"[22] to what is he referring? Or, what is really the same question, am I rigorously stereotyping Levertov—and by extension all women—when I find the immediate, sensual evocation of a personal, private experience to be what is best in her poetry; the analytic tendency to be a contradictory force? I believe that I am characterizing Levertov's art (and not merely my own preferences in art) in observing that when she comes closest to being involved and active in the experiences revealed by her poems, it is not in the role of observer or analyst, although for some people—Alexander Pope, for example—analysis might well be the most active mode! In the poems that deal with her personal experience, which tends to be particularly feminine in its nature (whether it be gathering in washing or encountering the Muse), she is most active, most participant, and most effective.

When one looks at her political poetry (that poetry which, according to tradition, ought to be the most public, the most "masculine"), this fact becomes clear.

Levertov has gathered her political poetry to 1971 in *To Stay Alive.*[23] This volume is composed primarily of a sequence of poems about Vietnam and the peace movement called *Staying Alive*, but it is preceded by *Preludes*, a section of earlier poems that in a sense prepared the way, for they were themselves a part of the process that they document, the growth of and coming to terms with political consciousness. The preludes begin with the "Olga poems," originally published in 1965. The nature of Levertov's political consciousness is indicated by the fact that these first political poems are an elegy for her sister, a sister who was, indeed, long before Denise Levertov, a political person.

The poems reveal Levertov trying to come to terms with her dead sister—particularly with the relationship that existed between them. Olga, the elder: fierce, passionate, anguished, dedicated, wanting "to change the course of the river" (iii); Denise, the younger: "the little sister / beady-eyed in the bed" (i), watching, following, not understanding, yet loving. The poems are a series of memories (meditations) about Olga, which constantly indicate the fascination of the elder sister for the younger as well as the accompanying disapproval:

> *Everything flows*
> she muttered into my childhood . . .
>
> I looked up from my Littlest Bear's cane armchair
> and knew the words came from a book
> and felt them alien to me
>
> (iii)

Many years of such observation allows her to characterize Olga with exquisite insight:

> . . . dread
> was in her, a bloodbeat, it was against the rolling dark
> oncoming river she raised bulwarks . . .
>
> (iii)

> Black one, incubus—
> she appeared
> riding anguish as Tartars ride mares
>
> over the stubble of bad years.
> (iii)

> Oh, in your torn stockings, with unwaved hair,
> you were trudging after your anguish
> over the bare fields, soberly, soberly.
> (v)

But it is when she encounters the fact of herself in Olga, Olga in herself, that the poem (which was written over a four-month period, from May to August 1964) draws together.

> As through a wood, shadows and light between birches,
> gliding a moment in open glades, hidden by thickets of holly
>
> your life winds in me.
> (v)

The final sequence of the poem focuses upon Olga's eyes, "the brown gold of pebbles underwater."

> . . . Even when we were estranged
> and my own eyes smarted in pain and anger at the thought of you.
> And by other streams in other countries; anywhere where the light
> reaches down through shallows to gold gravel. Olga's
> brown eyes.

She thinks of the fear in Olga's eyes, wonders how through it all "compassion's candle" kept alight in those eyes. The river that has become in the poem a symbol of the forces of time and history against which Olga had fought, in vain, or so it had always seemed to Denise ("to change, / to change the course of the river!") is now recognized as a part of the poet's life, too; and she wishes that she had understood more fully Olga's whiteness as well as her blackness ("Black one, black one, / there was a white / candle in your heart" [ii]).

I cross

so many brooks in the world, there is so much light
dancing on so many stones, so many questions my eyes
smart to ask of your eyes, gold brown eyes,
the lashes short but the lids
arched as if carved out of olivewood, eyes with some vision
of festive goodness in back of their hard, or veiled, or shining,
unknowable gaze . . .

(vi)

The poem's message to herself is clear: you can't only watch; you can't only remember; you must allow yourself to participate, to be touched.

In a poem like a postscript, "A Note to Olga (1966)," Levertov is describing her own participation in a peace march, the feeling she has of Olga's presence there, of the sound of Olga's hoarse voice somewhere in front of her, of the sense that it is Olga who is "lifted / limp and ardent" and carried off in a paddywagon. The poem begins with these lines:

Of lead and emerald
the reliquary
that knocks my breastbone,

slung round my neck
on a rough invisible rope
that rubs the knob of my spine.

Though I forget you
a red coal from your fire
burns in that box.

(i)

The reliquary is also not really there; neither is the coal; neither, in fact, is Olga there on the march. But the poet has incorporated the lesson that her own Olga poems had taught her: she has granted Olga access to her life and has entered Olga's, if only in retrospect or spirit.

The Olga poems are Levertov's first "political" poems, and she understands them to be so, because they reveal the first stirrings in her own mind of political consciousness in her attempt to come to terms with her "radical" sister Olga and with her own connection to Olga. A series of poems about Vietnam follow: poems justifiably well-known for their *human* approach to the war; for their concern with the Vietnamese as people who lead, in spite of/despite the war, ordinary, everyday lives; for their concern with Americans (and especially herself as an American) as human, too, and with their everyday lives during the condition that is war:

> And picnic parties return from the beaches
> burning with stored sun in the dusk;
> children promised a TV show when they get home
> fall asleep in the backs of a million station wagons,
> sand in their hair, the sound of waves
> quietly persistent at their ears.
> They are not listening.
> ("Tenebrae," fall of 1967)

The long poem, or sequence, *Staying Alive,* is a culmination of Levertov's concern with war and the times in the sixties, a concern that in this poem is related very specifically to her personal life, her own state of mind. A loose, journalistic form connects external events from the period—her husband's trial (he, along with Dr. Benjamin Spock and others, was accused of conspiracy), the People's Park episode in Berkeley (in which the attempt to make a park of university-owned land led to police intervention and brutality), trips to England, Europe, the Caribbean, two suicides, an antiwar fast, other actions of people who are important to her—to what she is feeling, thinking, writing about herself. What does she want, revolution or death? Where does life fit in? How can she live? How best be a poet? The events and the people around which the poem curves are all potential models, patterns; but the answer has to come from within herself:

> it's your well
>
> go deep into it
>
> into your own depths as into a poem
> (Part 3, ix)

In the author's preface to this volume, Levertov calls it "a record of one person's inner/outer experience in America during the '60's and the beginning of the '70's, an experience which is shared by so many and transcends the peculiar details of each life, though it can only be expressed in and through such details."[24] Her theory remains consistent, but the poems themselves are changing.

Staying Alive is different from many of her other poems in several significant ways. First, it is a *long* poem. Like the long poems of most other twentieth-century poets, it is really a sequence of short poems (because the unit of modern poetic discourse is the *moment* of perception), but these are nevertheless parts towards a whole. As moments of perception, the sections of *Staying Alive* all work towards the same end, towards a conclusion that unites them. As a long poem, the work is looser, more flexible in form than is usual for Levertov: prose, prose-poetry, long and short line units all have a place. (The form seems modeled upon that of Williams in *Paterson* or Pound in the *Cantos*, although Levertov makes no such grandiose claims for her long poem as the earlier writers did for theirs.) Finally, its thought patterns differ from her usual form, which tends to trace an experience in language (usually a circumscribed, personal experience) and to find its larger significance by relating that particular event to some concept: joy, love, the authentic. This poem appears to be working the other way around: beginning with the concepts—revolution, death; also war, life, happiness, achievement—and trying not merely to understand them but to come to terms with them, to participate in them, as they relate to particular events, as particular moments define or reveal or express them.

> What is the revolution I'm driven
> to name, to live in?—that now roars,
> a toneless constant, now
> sings itself?
>
> It's in the air: no air
> to breathe without
> scent of it,
> pervasive:
> odor of snow,
> freshwater,
> stink of damp
> vegetation recomposing.
> (Part 2)

People are experiences, also; so that throughout this poem people as they relate to the poet reveal revolution or death.

and still I've not begun the poem,
the one she asked for ("If you would write me a poem
I could live forever"—postmarked
the night she died, October twenty-ninth.)
I've begun though
to gather up fragments of it,
fragments of her: the heavy tarnished
pendant I don't wear,
the trapped dandelion seed in its transparent cube,
three notched green stones for divination, kept
in green velvet,
a set of the *Daily Californian* for all the days
of the struggle for the People's Park,
a thick folder of her letters,
and now (come with the Christmas mail, packed
in a pink cosmetic box grotesquely labelled,
"The Hope Chest"),
four cassettes recording (or so they are marked,
I've not played them) her voice speaking to me . . .

Revolution or death. She chose
as her life had long foretold . . .
("Two from the Fall Death-News")

Yet, finally, it is through herself that definitions come, through her personal experience. Characteristically, this experience is of both the physical, external world and the spiritual or internal world.

I like
my boots. I like
the warmth of my new long coat. Last winter
running through Cambridge with Boat and Richard, afraid of
the ice they
slid on fearlessly—I must have been cold all winter
without knowing it in my short light coat.
Buffalo Meat Market offers me a drink, (Strega),
I lug home
the ham for Christmas Eve, life
whirls its diamond sparklers before me.
Yes, I want

revolution, not death: but I don't
care about survival, I refuse
to be provident, to learn automechanics,
karate,
soybean cookery,
or how to shoot.
("Daily Life")

When he said
"Your struggle is my struggle"
a curtain was pushed away.

A curtain was pushed away revealing
an open window
and beyond that

an open country.
For the first time I knew it was actual.
("Revolutionary")

She was "indoors, still," she says, but the air from those fields "touched my face." The poet describes a country of hilly fields, shadows, and rivers, which she says have been hidden from her by a thick, heavy, dark curtain, "curtain of sorrow." In this vision, she also sees people moving far away:

struggling to move, as I
towards my window
struggle, burdened but not

each alone. They move
out in that air together
where I too

will be moving,
not alone.
("Revolutionary")

Only through an engagement with herself, both sensual and spiritual events show her, can she participate in the actions of others, can those actions have any meaning for her.

In *Staying Alive*, Levertov seems to me to be attempting, out of a feeling of genuine necessity, brought on by the intensely political situation that is living in modern America, to engage herself in her life and to engage her poetry in herself. She seems to feel that she has to, as a poet and a political person, in a way that she did not always feel she had to as a poet. Observing, sensitively recording what is seen is no longer enough—for this poem, for this book, at any rate. (The next book, *Footprints* [1972],[25] returns to her usual format, a collection of short, individual poems.)

I like *Staying Alive* because it *is* loose and experimental, because in it I think that Levertov does make use of her experience as a woman in the world in an exciting way. She commits herself to a force in her and in her poetry that is a powerful one and follows it through to a series of poems, a set of conclusions in a way that is not typical of her work as a whole.

Why does *To Stay Alive* happen? What is it about political poetry that occasions this breakthrough?

Levertov's notions about what it is to be political are learned to a large extent from a new generation of young women and anti-"masculine" young men (men who support love, peace, and feeling against war, aggressiveness, intellectualism): engagement and commitment are at the heart of their definition of the political. Her rules for art, on the other hand, come from an older tradition of poetry dominated by men who, while they were certainly not warmongers and, as men, were more feeling and sensitive than most, *i.e.*, poets, were nevertheless heirs to a masculine intellectual tradition of analysis and of the consequence and necessary condition of analysis—distance.

Feminine experience has, traditionally, demanded qualities of involvement in self and others, the same qualities that were appropriated, celebrated, seized upon by the antiwar activists of the sixties *because* they stood for the opposite of the forces being opposed: the exaggeratedly "masculine" tradition that had created an America that could be fighting such a war.

I think that when Levertov is writing nonpolitical poetry, the way in which she experiences the world as a woman (the way in which she has been socialized to experience but nevertheless *does* experience) is at odds with the form in which she has been taught to express, in language, that experience. When, on the other hand, she is writing expressly political poetry, her political aesthetics seem to reinforce her woman's experience, or vice versa, thereby creating a body of poems that have the strength of their consistency as a base for artistic success.

Her own talent for poetry complicates this neat dichotomy, because writing poetry is always more than a matter of rules and techniques; it is a matter, as she herself points out again and again, of unconscious forces at work upon the receptive mind of the poet as well as of the skill and labor required in expressing such forces in language. Thus Levertov's work contains a range of poems that vary in their emphases, their solutions, and their effectiveness.

NOTES

1. Robert Lowell, *Life Studies* (New York: Farrar, Straus and Cudahy, 1959).
2. *O Taste and See* (New York: New Directions, 1964), p. 9.
3. *The Poet in the World* (New York: New Directions, 1973), pp. 7–13.
4. *With Eyes at the Back of Our Heads* (New York: New Directions, 1959), p. 28.
5. *Footprints* (New York: New Directions, 1972), p. 16.
6. *The Sorrow Dance* (New York: New Directions, 1966), p. 79.
7. William Carlos Williams, *Autobiography* (New York: New Directions, 1951), p. 391.
8. *The Sorrow Dance*, p. 52.
9. "A Further Definition," *The Poet in the World*, p. 14.
10. "Some Notes on Organic Form," *The Poet in the World*, p. 12.
11. William Carlos Williams, *The Collected Earlier Poems* (New York: New Directions, 1951), p. 340.
12. "The Sense of Pilgrimage," *The Poet in the World*, p. 67.
13. "Origins of a Poem," *The Poet in the World*, p. 47.
14. "Some Notes on Organic Form," *The Poet in the World*, p. 13.
15. Ibid., p. 8.
16. "The Sense of Pilgrimage," *The Poet in the World*, p. 82.
17. "Origins of a Poem," *The Poet in the World*, p. 43.
18. Poems specifically about women's experience: *The Jacob's Ladder*: "Song for a Dark Voice," "The Thread," "From the Roof," "Matins"; *O Taste and See*: "The Ache of Marriage," "Love Song," "Eros at Temple Stream," "About Marriage," "Hypocrite Women," "In Mind," "Our Bodies," "Losing Track," "A Psalm Praising the Hair of Man's Body"; *The Sorrow Dance*: "Abel's Bride," "Face to Face," "Stepping Westward," "Bedtime," "The Son," "Hymn to Eros," "The Mutes," "Olga Poems"; *Relearning the Alphabet*: "What Wild Dawns There Were," "Waiting," "Mad Song," "Keeping Track," "He-Who-Came-

Forth"; *Footprints*: "A Defeat in the Green Mountains," "Love Poem," "The Poem Unwritten," "Brass Tacks"; *To Stay Alive* as a whole.

19. *The Jacob's Ladder* (New York: New Directions, 1961), p. 49.
20. "The Sense of Pilgrimage," *The Poet in the World*, p. 77.
21. Ibid., pp. 77–78.
22. Quoted on the dustjacket of *The Jacob's Ladder* from *The New York Times Book Review*.
23. *To Stay Alive* (New York: New Directions, 1971).
24. "Author's Preface," Ibid., p. ix.
25. *Footprints* (New York: New Directions, 1972).

5

"The Blood Jet": The Poetry of Sylvia Plath

"The only good poetess is a dead"

The quote is from Erica Jong's poem about being a woman poet, "Bitter Pills for the Dark Ladies."[1] That poem is prefaced with a quotation from Robert Lowell's foreword to Plath's *Ariel*: "—hardly a person at all, or woman, certainly not another 'poetess,' but . . ." Lowell's remark is worth looking at in its entirety, because, although confusing, it represents one of the most common of the prevailing attitudes towards Sylvia Plath.

> In these poems, written in the last months of her life and often rushed out at the rate of two or three a day, Sylvia Plath becomes herself, becomes something imaginary, newly, wildly and subtly created—hardly a person at all, or a woman, certainly not another "poetess," but one of those super-real, hypnotic, great classical heroines. This character is feminine, rather than female, though almost everything we customarily think of as feminine is turned on its head.[2]

I need to talk about prevailing attitudes when I write about Plath, because such strong ones exist, and that fact alone is significant. For many, the most important fact about Plath is that she is dead; that she killed herself at the age of thirty-one. She had to die as she did in order to get the kind of recognition that Lowell gives to her. The fact of her death has allowed her to be appreciated and even venerated as a wonderfully sensitive soul who transcended life by death and art; a myth; a prophetess. Certainly not a woman; "hardly a person at all." The particular, real issues and experiences with which her last poems deal, issues and experiences that shaped her life and occasioned her death, the forms and techniques that she found for handling and expressing these issues and experiences, these need not concern or threaten anyone.

Yet the anticult, purely literary approach to Plath as a poet arrives, in its own way, at similar ends. Handling her characters as imaginative creations and not "real people," treating her voice as that of a persona and not Plath "herself," can lead to conclusions such as these of Charles Newman, who is, it is interesting to note, talking about both Plath and Dickinson:

> Both cut through popular sociology by acknowledging the terrifying ambiguity of the female role, and then by universalizing their very feminism. That is to say, by rejecting the traditional pose of the "heroine" they give us the woman as "hero"—a protagonist who not only undergoes the central action of a work, but a character whom men as well as women may view as an actor in a destiny possible for them.[3]

While it is always true that art transforms experience, that the poetic persona (the voice that speaks the poem) is not the voice that phones the baby-sitter but is rather a projection, a creation based upon the self, it does not follow that the poet who writes of herself is not in the poem or that the experience of which she writes is not in the poem. It also does not follow that for the experience to be profound and "worthy" of a great literary protagonist it must become universal or must transcend sex. Plath's life and art seem to me to be wholly connected to the fact that she was a woman poet; for various reasons to be discussed, she is the most extreme instance of this situation that I know.

Newman, as an admirer of Plath, is reacting against one other mode of interpretation, however: that which classes her as a "confessional" poet and therefore, by definition, as not capable of producing great literature because she is writing about personal, private experience.

> Sylvia Plath's range of technical resources was narrower than Robert Lowell's, and so, apparently, was her capacity for intellectual objectivity. As a highly organized woman, intensely absorbed by her children and by the emotional problems of her marriage . . . the path she took as a

> poet was perhaps predictable. She chose, if that is the word, what seems to me the one alternative advance position to Lowell's along the dangerous confessional way, that of literally committing her own predicaments in the interests of her art until the one was so involved in the other that no return was possible. It was the old romantic fallacy, if you will, of confusing motive and art, or the real with the ideal. But in this instance the conception has no real meaning because the long, escalating drive towards suicide and the period of extraordinary creativity (comparable in its way to the brief, miraculous period of Keats's most fruitful writing) actually coincided, or were at least two functions of the same process.[4]

M. L. Rosenthal's not-so-implicit assumption is that as a woman, someone not as capable of "intellectual objectivity" as the male poet to whom she is being compared, someone whose range of experience is in itself trivial—children, the emotional problems of marriage—Plath not only chooses a minor mode in which to write but pulls it off badly: she can't even see the difference between art and life! Lowell, on the other hand, not only writes about more inherently important personal experiences (*his* mental breakdown? *his* father? *his* marriage?), but he is capable of objectifying art, of distancing himself from himself and from his poems. In other words, he doesn't kill himself. As for Keats, the other male poet to whom Rosenthal refers, he also did not kill himself; he died of tuberculosis. His surge of creativity before death is called "brief and miraculous," while Plath's is called a long, escalating drive along the "dangerous, confessional way."

The primary fact remains that as a living poet, Plath never received the intense reaction, be it eulogy or damnation, that her death provoked (although many of the poems in the *Ariel* volume were either being published, or rejected, by periodicals during her lifetime). Her last poems were then and are now frightening, and very good; they ought to hurt and are meant to hurt. Yet the fact of her death has enabled readers and critics to handle them in an anesthetized way. Because she is dead, no one need feel the blame or the responsibility that these poems engender.

In my own reaction to and analysis of the poetry of Sylvia Plath, I would, however, in no way discount her death. It is of supreme importance, surely, because it is to that death that both her life and her art led her. A life and art that were by definition different from one another but intimately related, ultimately interdependent.

"When on tiptoe the schoolgirls danced"

Unlike Sexton, because she came to poetry so late, or Levertov, who usually evades the problem, Plath suffered in an extreme form from the woman artist's need to reconcile her two roles, woman and poet; from the necessity of living with what may seem her two selves. The exaggerated nature of her situation and her suffering seems to have resulted from the peculiar temporal and social context in which Plath's life and art grew: the fifties, New England, the middle class. Sylvia Plath as high school and college superachiever, the prettiest, the most popular, *and* the smartest, with her dark-red lipsticked smile, her carefully waved hair, a perfection of surfaces, was in discord with another "self": the poet whose words could destroy surfaces and open inner places, inner wounds, inner emptiness.

Roles are not really selves, although they may seem so to the person enacting them. To talk about the conflict Plath experienced as woman and poet, as body and mind, is not to talk in the jargon of psychiatry about split personalities and pathological mental states. Role conflicts occur in everyone; but if they are too extreme and too prolonged they can surely have unpleasant consequences, especially if the conflict occurs between roles so primary to the personality that neither can be readily eliminated. I think that Plath's suffering was caused by such a role conflict and by the measures she took at various stages of her life to try to ease the strain.

In high school, Plath seems to have swallowed whole the myth of the All-Round Student and projected it back to the world as only one so capable and thorough as she could do, achieving a perfection of the role. She played tennis, was on the girls' basketball team, was an editor of the school newspaper, was a sorority member, painted decorations for class dances, went on college weekends, acted in the class play.[5] At the time she was also writing, and taking that as seriously as she took everything else about herself: she had sent forty-five pieces to *Seventeen* before the acceptance in March 1950 of a short story. The tale continued at Smith College: scholarships, awards, and prizes of all kinds came to her, seemingly for the asking.

There is no need to document the existence and kind of pressure exerted by society upon adolescent women to prepare for and to begin to assume their roles as sexual beings. There is also no need to take sides in the debate that often occurs between the pretty girls and the smart girls as to who had it worse. They both did. What is necessary to point out here is that for the bright young woman, and especially in American high schools of the fifties, there was only one way to validate the possession of an intellect: by proving that one was as pretty and as popular and as "normal" as anyone else (for normal meant, of course, pretty and popular). Plath seems to have pulled it off "exceptionally well." (The quote is from her poem "Lady Lazarus" and refers to her skill at dying. But that came later.) Having proved her normalcy (femininity), she could also pursue scholarly activities. She was, after all, still in school; and schools, if not peers, reward success in such endeavors.

Yet college was interrupted by the depression and suicide attempt that she made famous in her novel (written a good many years afterwards), *The Bell Jar*.

> I felt dreadfully inadequate. The trouble was, I had been inadequate all along, I simply hadn't thought about it.
>
> The one thing I was good at was winning scholarships and prizes, and that era was coming to an end.[6]

> I hadn't washed my hair for three weeks, either.
>
> I hadn't slept for seven nights. . . .
>
> The reason I hadn't washed my clothes or my hair was because it seemed so silly.
>
> I saw the days of the year stretching ahead like a series of bright, white boxes, and separating one box from another was sleep, like a black shade. Only for me, the long perspective of shades that set off one box from the next had suddenly snapped up, and I could see day after day glaring ahead of me like a white, broad, infinitely desolate avenue.
>
> It seemed silly to wash one day when I would only have to wash again the next.
>
> It made me tired just to think of it.
>
> I wanted to do everything once and for all and be through with it.[7]

The Bell Jar is a writer's attempt to understand and to analyze her own mental condition: it is interpretive, but it does nevertheless point to certain elements of the situation that help explain why at precisely this moment the gears that were working at such top speed came to a grinding halt for a while. A feeling of insecurity, puzzling to many who knew only the surface Sylvia Plath, is documented also in her letters and confidences of the period: "for the few little outward successes I may seem to have, there are acres of misgivings and self-doubt."[8]

There are overtones of both false modesty and adolescent exaggeration here, but the feeling that prompts the statement seems genuine. And understandable, given the conflict she must have experienced between her long devotion to maintaining that surface perfection and her doubts about its validity—and even its reality.

The overt "symptoms" of her depression, not washing her clothing or her hair, not keeping up her feminine appearance, not keeping up appearances, send a clear message to the world: I have stopped playing my role. Why? Because, as the passage I have quoted reveals, another vision has interfered with, has short-circuited the dictates of society. It is a vision of life as a prison of bright meaninglessness; a vision of her own life as she had been busy creating it. A life that from her changed perspective hardly seems worth the trouble. The vision was not sent to her; it came from within herself, from a part of herself she had been carefully ignoring because such a penetrating kind of insight could destroy her all-important surfaces. It has already begun to do so by forcing her to question those ritual acts of hair-washing, dressing well—of looking pretty. The vision leads to an attempt at death, at "being through with it."

Yet when the suicide attempt proves abortive, and after the care of the psychiatrists, Plath seems to get back on the track. She finishes Smith with glory, goes off for two postgraduate years at Cambridge, marries a rising young British poet, and returns to America to teach at Smith, carrying out her program for success with her old skill and determination. It is from this period (1955–1959) that the poems of her first book, *The Colossus*, come.[9]

"And heart's frosty discipline / Exact as a snowflake"

"She wrote her early poems very slowly," writes her husband, Ted Hughes. "Thesaurus open on her knee, in her large, strange handwriting, like a mosaic, where every letter stands separate within the work, a hieroglyph to itself."[10] This is a glittery, brilliant, self-conscious poetry of surfaces, a cold poetry: Sylvia Plath's diamond gift to the world. Commentators on the verse of *The Colossus* are always picking out influences, naming Theodore Roethke, Wallace Stevens, D. H. Lawrence, Dylan Thomas. Certainly they are there, for this is the poetry of a woman who has studied hard in the school of modern poetry and, as in everything, always, learned her lessons well. She observes the world around her and claims it as her own by imposing order, the order of language, upon it. She has an eye, an ear:

> The pears fatten like little buddhas.
> ("The Manor Garden")

> In their jars the snail-nosed babies moon and glow.
> He hands her the cut-out heart like a cracked heirloom.
> ("Two Views of a Cadaver Room")

> . . . This vast
> Brobdingnag bulk
>
> Of a sow lounged belly-bedded on that black compost,
> Fat-rutted eyes
> Dream-filmęd
> ("Sow")

> They're out of the dark's ragbag, these two
> Moles dead in the pebbled rut,
> Shapeless as flung gloves. . . .
> ("Blue Moles")

She has, as well, a vision: the perception of the worm in every apple core that breeds in her a bitter humor, a delight in the knowledge of disintegration and death. These elements give a focus to her observations:

> These three, unmasked now, bear
> Dry witness
> To the gross eating game
> We'd wink at if we didn't hear
> Stars grinding, crumb by crumb,
> Our own grist down to its bony face.
> ("All the Dead Dears")

Yet the vision seems often precocious. Precocious because it expresses knowledge without experience. Perhaps my impression is wrong; yet if experience exists, it is not allowed into the poems. The poet is at all times detached from her subject.

"Man in Black," for example, a poem that contains the death motif central to all of Plath's poetry, is essentially a landscape. The poet as watcher creates a scene. She first dissects it into its components; then she reassembles it, having found its fulcrum, its significance as a unit of *related* elements. The components of this scene are rocks ("three magenta / Breakwaters" that "take the shove / And suck of the grey sea / To the left"), the sea ("the wave / Unfists against the dun / Barbwired headland"), an island prison ("The Deer Island Prison / With its trim piggeries, / Hen huts and cattle green / To the right"), ice, rock pools, and cliffs:

> . . . and March ice
> Glazes the rock pools yet,
> Snuff-colored sand cliffs rise
>
> Over a great stone spit
> Bared by each falling tide

Finally, a man:

> And you, across those white
>
> Stones, strode out in your dead
> Black coat, black shoes, and your
> Black hair till there you stood. . . .

We might assume that the man is the human element in the scene, but the language describing him divests him of his humanity. He is further dissected into components—coat, shoes, hair, not a whole man; and he is black, dead. The natural world, on the other hand, is vital and active: the sea shoves and sucks, the wave is a fist, the ice acts upon the rock pools, glazing them, the cliffs rise, each falling tide bares the stone spit. Yet the man is nevertheless the focus of the scene, its "fixed vortex," so that the word around which the poem turns is the "till" in the final line just quoted: "till there you stood,"

> Fixed vortex on the far
> Tip, riveting stones, air,
> All of it, together.

The man walks out on the stone and then stops. Then his negativity, his absence of life, makes sense of the March landscape, stills its frenetic energy, rivets, fixes it into stasis: the stasis already implicit in its iciness, its bareness—the stasis of death. (When I read this poem, I always think that the man is about to commit suicide. Yet that is surely beside the point; not only because such an action is outside the poem, but because he is in some sense dead already. This is a poem about death in life.) It is of course Plath's perception of the death elements in man and in nature that allows her to compose the scene as she does, so to say that she is absent from the poem is wrong. But her participation is external, as it is in most of her poems about scenes from nature or society, the majority of the poems in *The Colossus*. What is most important about poems such as "Man in Black" is the element of control that they manifest: a firm and skillful control over language that results in control over the external world. Having divided it into its component parts and then reassembled those elements according to her own concept of order, they belong to her and therefore (hopefully) do not threaten. (In a memorial essay, A. Alvarez postulates that what "made her write" was "an underlying sense of violent unease," and that "it took a great deal of efficiency to keep it in check.")[11] It is understandable that a person who sees division, separation in her very self, who is morbidly conscious of surfaces and interiors and of the gap between the two, will be aware of corresponding states in the external world. At this stage in her poetic development, she seems to believe in the power of her own will to control the world, even as she kept herself in control through the same kind of effort.

Not all of the poems of *The Colossus* are about nature; at times the poet herself is a major actor in the narrative. But always the principles of objectivity and distance are fundamental. For example, in "Two Views of a Cadaver Room," the personal experience, that of visiting a dissecting room, is neatly balanced against a description of a Brueghel canvas. The title makes the connection: both are versions of the human condition—the world is one big cadaver room!

Even in Part 1, the "personal" experience, Plath acts as detached observer, describing with imagistic if not clinical detail the four bodies, "black as burnt turkey, / Already half unstrung"; the medical students, "the white-smocked boys"; one cadaver in particular, held together by "a sallow piece of string," a "rubble of skull plates and old leather"; and the fetuses in jars, "the snail-nosed babies" that "moon and glow." When she is forced into physical contact with the "cut-out heart," she describes it as being presented to her like "a cracked heirloom," thereby commenting upon the student's pride in his work, work that she, however, considers both ominous and ludicrous. Such is the effect of the images she creates, which are oblique reports of her reactions, opinions.

When she turns to "Brueghel's panorama of smoke and slaughter," she concentrates upon the only two people in the canvas who are "blind to the carrion army"—two lovers, lost in blue satin skirts, music, and one another: "deaf to the fiddle in the hands / Of the death's head shadowing their song." Again, the sense of the ludicrousness of human life, now attempting love (as before, in the cadaver room, attempting knowledge or salvation) in the face of prevailing death, is omnipresent, and is driven home with a flourish of irony in the concluding couplet:

> Yet desolation, stalled in paint, spares the little country
> Foolish, delicate, in the lower right-hand corner.

Only art, which is *not*, the poet points out, reality ("stalled in paint"), can keep alive such a moment, a moment delicate but ultimately foolish.

Even in a poem like "The Colossus," in which the poet is exploring a very private, very personal experience, her relationship with her dead father, whom she both adores and hates because he died, because he is dead and still influences her life, she needs at this point in her career to generalize, even mythicize the experience to control it and therefore to write about it. (From later poems on the theme, such as "Daddy," we get a clearer picture of the devastating strength of her emotions. But in this poem they are modulated by their symbolic form.)

The father is seen as a great but broken statue, a ruin from some former time: "O father, all by yourself / You are pithy and historical as the Roman Forum." The poet is laboring, as she has been for thirty years, she says, to get him "put together entirely / Pieced, glued, and properly jointed"—to bring him back to life or to put him into perspective, either way means freeing herself from his power. Plath's characteristic irony (yet another method of distancing) is here directed upon herself:

> Scaling little ladders with gluepots and pails of lysol
> I crawl like an ant in morning
> Over the weedy acres of your brow
> To mend the immense skull plates and clear
> The bald, white tumuli of your eyes.

This strange scene is put into its "proper" context: "A blue sky out of the Oresteia / Arches above us." There is again the mockery: we are like some characters out of a Greek drama, not *real* people at all; but there is also the epic dimension that the vision gives to these actors. The poet is not only Sylvia Plath, she is a type of Electra, the daughter who avenged the murder of her father, Agamemnon. They become more than themselves when identified with the devoted daughter/dead father archetype. Finally, the very setting itself helps to supply the bitter "moral" of the story:

> Nights, I squat in the cornucopia
> Of your left ear, out of the wind,
>
> Counting the red stars and those of plum-color.
> The sun rises under the pillar of your tongue.
> My hours are married to shadow.
> No longer do I listen for the scrape of a keel
> On the blank stones of the landing.

The scene, being a symbolic construction, is meant to be translated into a psychological and emotional vocabulary: I am yoked, dedicated to death, observes the protagonist. The giant statue is mythic and larger than life, but in being so it is also the past—it is irrevocably dead and cannot be reconstructed. But it has become her only home. She lives in its shadow and views the living world from its perspective. Her own life, as she sees it, is therefore a living death.

One poem in the volume, however, "The Disquieting Muses," is to some degree different from those I have been discussing. Like the others, it transposes personal drama onto a more "objective" level: in this case, to the realm of fairy tales. It externalizes elements from her own psyche, her poetic impulses or vision, into three ladies, three evil fairies, three disquieting muses. But this poem nevertheless resolutely attempts to describe, to reveal that aspect of self: the very one that is being suppressed or certainly harnessed in poems like "Man in Black," "Two Views of a Cadaver Room," or "The Colossus"—the one that led her to try, at nineteen, to kill herself. Perhaps because of its difference in approach, the poem's language is different, too: both more narrative and less image-laden, less baroque.

> Mother, mother, what illbred aunt
> Or what disfigured and unsightly

Cousin did you so unwisely keep
Unasked to my christening, that she
Sent these ladies in her stead
With heads like darning-eggs to nod
And nod and nod at foot and head
And at the left side of my crib?

In the first stanza, explicit analogy sets up what will be the underlying allegory for the poem: Plath is a Sleeping Beauty, and contesting for her soul are her real mother (to whom the poem is addressed) and three evil fairies. The language of the first stanza concentrates upon the narrative, so that the one figure of speech, "heads like darning-eggs," is especially dramatic with its image of smooth vacancy.

Mother and godmothers are vying to teach the princess the "correct" lessons. Fairy tales are themselves one form in which lessons come. Her mother is on the side of goodness, of happy endings: "Mother, who made to order stories / Of Mixie Blackshort the heroic bear, / Mother, whose witches always, always / Got baked into gingerbread." But she is not, in Plath's view, on the side of reality. Reality is the not-always-welcome christening gift of the three ladies "Nodding by night around my bed, / Mouthless, eyeless, with stitched bald head." Again the second stanza, the one figure of speech, an elaboration of the darning-egg comparison, heightens the terrifying silence of the fairies in contrast to the garrulous mother.

The next three stanzas demonstrate the dark powers of the three ladies, who by their very passive being sabotage the energetic work of the mother. During a hurricane, for example, the mother supplies Ovaltine and cookies and optimistic magical chants (" 'Thor is angry: boom boom boom! / Thor is angry: we don't care!' ") in the face of real, albeit symbolic, destruction: "But those ladies broke the panes." Again, "when on tiptoes the schoolgirls danced," the speaker could not lift a foot in her twinkle-dress in the shadows cast by the "dismal-headed / Godmothers," although her mother cried and cried: "And the shadow stretched, and the lights / Went out." At piano lessons, although praised by her mother, she was tone-deaf: "I learned, I learned, I learned elsewhere. / From muses unhired by you, dear mother."

In each of these episodes, the forced brightness and lightness of the mother is counterweighted by the concluding line or lines of the stanza, which pronounce the power of the three Muses. These lessons in dance and music are of course counterparts to the warfare over the mind and soul of the "princess," as she saw it being waged.

This terse personal history is concluded by a vision of the final defeat of the mother, a vision surely inspired by the three Muses, the very forces that brought about the defeat. The mother's fairy-tale mentality and philosophy are physically embodied in a scene whose bright and happy colors are belied by its complete resignation and bleakness of outlook.

> I woke one day to see you, mother,
> Floating above me in bluest air
> On a green balloon bright with a million
> Flowers and bluebirds that never were
> Never, never, found anywhere.
> But the little planet bobbed away
> Like a soap-bubble as you called: Come here!
> And I faced my travelling companions.

The reality principle has been invoked with finality. Your vision of life was a dream, mother, says the poet: a soap-bubble, a never-never land that is not real. And you are part of it, mother; you aren't real, either. What are real, the final line indicates, are my "travelling companions." I go with them because they have become me and I them, they are inside of me, they are me.

> Day now, night now, at head, side, feet,
> They stand their vigil in gowns of stone,
> Faces blank as the day I was born,
> Their shadows long in the setting sun
> That never brightens or goes down.
> And this is the kingdom you bore me to,
> Mother, mother. But no frown of mine
> will betray the company I keep.

Here is yet another vision of death, a spiritual death that the poem transforms into a physical one. The godmothers who stood by the cradle with their christening wish have achieved their prophecy as they stand, carved angels, by the tomb. Theirs is the kingdom of death. But of course the speaker is not *really* dead, she is speaking the poem. Then what is this death that she is living, a state characterized by shadow and blankness on the part of both Muses and poet (for her face, like theirs, has become totally expressionless, hiding their existence inside her, their presence from the outside world)? It is the state in which she can make poetry: for these evil fairies are her Muses, and the gift they have given her is the power to see the real. The real is disquieting—frightening, because it contains within itself at all times the existence of death; but the ability to see the real is the price this poet must pay for the ability to make poems. What sort of poems will the poet possessing such Muses make? Either true poems, or false poems. The false ones come when the poet is frightened of the very vision that has provoked them; when she obscures that vision like a cat covering its feces by throwing up little mounds of words around it, by attempting through cleverness and wit and above all distance to make it presentable to the world—not *dirty*. True poems occur when she can (and will) write what she sees: when the words make happen on paper what is happening inside her. The final two stanzas of "The Disquieting Muses," the visions of her mother disappearing and of the Muses at the tomb of herself, come close to this kind of truth, although the poem as a whole does not. It is still too essayistic, talking about a condition rather than enacting it; it remains too indebted in technique to the fine art of feces-obscuring. But for me it stands as a first step on the way to the later poems, because it does attempt to talk about the force that has been carefully hidden inside herself ("no frown of mine" betraying its existence) for many years: the force that will produce the exceptional poetry of her last years.

"I may be ugly and hairy"

In the final three years of her life (1960–1963), Sylvia Plath gave up her plans to be a professor of literature and turned completely to writing poetry, settled in England, gave birth to two children, separated from her husband, and twice attempted suicide. During this period, she wrote what is in my opinion a different kind of poetry: a poetry that at last manifested the reality of her experience as a woman and poet.

"She is a very different woman in the last long year of her life," writes her critic and admirer, Charles Newman. "Photographs at the time indicate that she had lost all resemblance to the Smith girl who won the *Mademoiselle* fiction contest. She is deliberately dowdy, hyper-English, very much the mother and established poetess."[12] Everyone who writes about her during this period, in whatever context, notices a change. A. Alvarez links the change in her poetry to the birth of her children:

> The *real* poems began in 1960, after the birth of her daughter, Frieda. It is as though the child were a proof of her identity, as though it liberated her into her real self. I think this guess is borne out by the fact that her most creative period followed the birth of her son, two years later.[13]

(The "creative period" to which Alvarez refers is the two or three months before her death, during which time she wrote one, two, or even three poems a day, every day, up until the day she died.) The change in appearance seems linked in some way to the change in the poetry itself, a change that Alvarez relates to "identity" and "real self." Since surfaces had been throughout her life of the utmost importance to her, the fact that her surface appearance had altered is not at all trivial. Esther Greenwood of *The Bell Jar*, as we have seen, in refusing to wash her hair or change her clothes, is rejecting a complete and carefully cultivated image of herself, her role as American Girl, the Great Virgin Sex Queen. But to appear drab and dowdy is not, I do not think, to take on another surface, another role, that of the British "Mum." It is rather a negation of surfaces: it is to not do the work, to reject the feminine body by refusing to anoint and decorate and worship it. It is, in consequence, to reject the body-as-object as she herself had created it:

> A living doll, everywhere you look.
> It can sew, it can cook,
> It can talk, talk, talk.
> It works, there is nothing wrong with it.
> ("The Applicant")[14]

In a thinly veiled allegory about her perception of her "two selves," "In Plaster" (March 1961),[15] a poem describing a woman wearing a cast, Plath comments upon the relation between the surface woman and the one "inside."

> . . . There are two of me now:
> This new absolutely white person and the old yellow one.

The surface woman, the plaster woman, is cold, white, beautiful, tidy, calm, patient, and thinks she is "immortal." At first the woman inside is kind to the plaster woman: "I realized what she wanted was for me to love her":

> Without me, she wouldn't exist, so of course she was grateful.
> I gave her a soul, I bloomed out of her as a rose
> Blooms out of a vase of not very valuable porcelain.

Then she realizes that a death struggle is going on between the two of them:

> She wanted to leave me, she thought she was superior,
> And I'd been keeping her in the dark, and she was resentful—
> Wasting her days waiting on a half-corpse!
> And secretly she began to hope I'd die.
> Then she could cover my mouth and eyes, cover me entirely,
> And wear my painted face the way a mummy-case
> Wears the face of a pharaoh, though it's made of mud and water.

The inner woman's problem is that she has grown dependent upon the surface woman: "She's supported me for so long I was quite limp."

> Living with her was like living with my own coffin:
> Yet I still depended on her, though I did it regretfully.

In the final stanza, the inner woman is plotting her revolution:

> I used to think we might make a go of it together—
> After all, it was a kind of marriage, being so close.
> Now I see it must be one or the other of us.
> She may be a saint, and I may be ugly and hairy,
> But she'll soon find out that that doesn't matter a bit.
> I'm collecting my strength; one day I shall manage without her,
> And she'll perish with emptiness then, and begin to miss me.

As a poem, this narrative remains grounded in its allegorical mechanics, but as a piece of self-analysis its perceptions bear out my own observations about the existence and nature of the role conflict that Plath had been experiencing all of her life and of her decision during this period to resolve it. She had decided to place her faith in the inner woman, "the old yellow one," because she had seen with an overwhelming clarity that the cold and perfect surface woman was an illusion. Certainly the struggle between them had been destructive, but now she would annihilate once and for all that cold, sterile woman/

body/object self and give freedom to her creative impulses and vision, the "inner" self.

Her change in appearance follows Plath's rejection of America, her rejection of the profession for which she had been in training most of her life: that of teacher/scholar. She chooses, instead, England, poetry, and motherhood. She chooses another body image, which seems to be a more suitable vessel for her mind and soul. Another form for woman: no longer sex object but mother; no longer the narcissistic sterility of surfaces, but the nurturant fertility of inner spaces, of the womb. Her woman's creativity (children) and her poet's creativity (poems) will coincide and correspond, and she will no longer be two warring selves but one whole person: the woman poet. In the process, she rejects as unreal all surfaces, all externals, even as she affirms the inside rather than the outside of her body. The poetry of this period reflects her attitude: in it, objects from the external world are meaningful only as they define her own consciousness. She pulls the outer world inside her mind, inside her poetry.

Her decision (whether "conscious" or "unconscious" is really irrelevant, since what we as readers deal with are its results) to commit herself to poetry and thus to her own poetic vision resulted in an engagement with her poetry (a participation and an involvement) that had been missing from her earlier work. Her husband comments on this kind of involvement by saying that "she had none of the usual guards and remote controls to protect herself from her own reality. She lived right in it, especially during the last two years of her life. Perhaps that is one of the privileges, or the prices, of being a woman and at the same time an initiate into the poetic order of events."[16]

It is indicative of her new ability to "live right in" these poems that they, unlike the earlier ones, were meant to be read aloud, as Plath remarks in an interview and reading of poems that she did for the British Council:

> I have found myself having to read them aloud to myself. Now this is something I didn't do. For example, my first book, *The Colossus*—I can't read any of the poems aloud now. I didn't write them to be read aloud. In fact, they quite privately bore me. Now these very recent ones—I've got to say them. I speak them to myself.[17]

These poems were no longer carefully plotted with the thesaurus; they came more directly from inside herself.

For Plath, poetry had always been symbolic action. In *The Colossus,* she had used language to impose an order upon experience, but the order in her poems contradicted her vision of reality as fragmented and perpetually disintegrating. Only in a poem could the world be composed and controlled, and so poetry was artificial; it lied. In the later poetry, she begins to tell the truth. When she comes to see that reality resides in her own mind, words and poems become as real as anything else. The expression of her vision in words unleashes reality, for her poems describe what is real: her own consciousness. The action that is poetry is recognized as symbolic action (she never ceases to know the *difference* between art and life), but the symbols now reflect rather than counteract her own life.

The poems of these final years render in symbolic action her personal battle between life and death. It appears that in committing herself to her artistic and bodily creativity, she had not alleviated the struggle but rather had heightened it. First, because the positive values of motherhood were outweighed in her life by its negative ones.

There may have been, for a short while at least (during pregnancy, right after birth), a respite from the long conflict between body and mind, woman and poet, that had plagued her for so many years.

> When I walk out, I am a great event.
> I do not have to think, or even rehearse.
> What happens in me will happen without attention.
> The pheasant stands on the hill;
> He is arranging his brown feathers.
> I cannot help smiling at what I know.
> Leaves and petals attend me. I am ready.

So the voice of the mother in Plath's lengthy exploration of maternity, *Three Women (Crossing the Water),* describes the condition of unity between one's own body and the body of the world that the woman entering into childbirth feels.

But when pregnancy and childbirth are over, what is left is the child. Children, especially infants, are uncompromisingly loving and trusting, but they present two major problems. First, one spends more time cleaning and feeding and cleaning them than simply loving them: "Meanwhile there's a stink of fat and baby crap" ("Lesbos"). The late poems were all written before 8:00 A.M., during the early morning hours before the children woke and her life as a mother (rather than poet) began. The conflict had surely returned in another form. The second problem with children is that one cannot keep them: slowly, from birth, the mother watches her perfect creation corrupted from her by the world that has already corrupted herself. The song of the mother in *Three Women* that follows is echoed again and again in her poems of mother love.

> How long can I be a wall, keeping the wind off?
> How long can I be
> Gentling the sun with the shade of my hand,
> Intercepting the blue bolts of a cold moon?
> The voices of loneliness, the voices of sorrow
> Lap at my back ineluctably.
> How shall it soften them, this little lullaby?

The two kinds of creativity are not the same; there remains a gap between woman and poet.

As poet, Plath sees with increasing clarity this gap. She sees as well the existence of life and its inevitable corruption into death. The forces in her that gave rise to her awareness of and fascination with death are surely complex; but surely the fact that she existed for so long with a sense of her own self as disparate, bifurcated, contributed to a desire for wholeness that she could equate only with death. The pulse of life was the movement towards disintegration: the stasis of death brought integration. And perfection. For Plath had viewed perfection as a solution to her problem, a perfection that she had been led to believe was achievable through talent and sheer willpower. She needed to be good at everything because in that way she could *be* everything: woman and poet. Although this program proved impossible, she was left with a belief in, and a desire to achieve, perfection. There was perfection in death.

The nature of her struggle between the forces of life and death is revealed in the vocabulary as well as the themes of her poetry. Blood, flowers, babies, pain, cries, and breath form image clusters (units of experience) that compete for Plath's favors with emptiness, purity, colorlessness, perfection, stars, moon, and snow; with "the cold dead center / Where spilt lives congeal and stiffen to history" ("A Birthday Present"). Poetry, "the blood jet," starts in life but moves towards death: "there is no stopping it" ("Kindness").

"The woman is perfected"

A selection of poems from the last nine months of Plath's life was published posthumously in 1965 by her husband in *Ariel.* In 1971 more poems appeared: *Winter Trees,*[18] containing more of the final poems, and *Crossing the Water,* transitional poems from the period between *The Colossus* and the *Ariel* poems. It was *Ariel* that caused Plath's fame, her myth. For whatever else these poems were (or seemed to be), they were and are fully realized, powerful, and vital.

The themes of these last poems all intertwine. There are poems concerned with varied aspects of womanhood, such as "Lesbos," "Childless Woman," "The Munich Mannequins," *Three Women*; the particular experience of motherhood, such as "Nick and the Candlestick," "You're," "Child"; emotional life and fantasies, such as "Letter in November," "Daddy," "Kindness"; nature (which is, however, as much emotional life and fantasy as anything else), such as "Sheep in Fog," "Ariel," "The Moon and the Yew Tree"; the life-death battle, a primary element in the emotional and fantasy life, such as "Tulips," "Death & Co.," "Edge"; and a myth for the life-death battle, the bee poems, "The Bee Meeting," "The Arrival of the Bee Box," and so forth. The themes are so intertwined because all are manifestations of the consciousness of Sylvia Plath. The struggle between life and death may not always be the ostensible or overt subject of a poem, but the perceptions and ideas of a consciousness that is struggling between life and death not only color but indeed control the vision of every poem produced.

The image clusters mentioned earlier contribute to the unity of vision and form that these poems achieve. Plath's poetic vocabulary is always value-laden: words like "white" or "red," "moon" or "heart" carry with them a set of symbolic associations whenever they appear, creating both emotional and conceptual resonances and meanings.

Life: blood, flowers, babies, love, red, pain, cries, breath.

> The chimneys of the city breathe, the window sweats,
> The children leap in their cots.
> The sun blooms, it is a geranium.
>
> The heart has not stopped.
>
> ("Mystic," *Winter Trees*)

> The blood blooms clean

In you, ruby.

. . . . .

Love, love,
I have hung our cave with roses.

. . . .

You are the one
solid the spaces lean on, envious.
You are the baby in the barn.
("Nick and the Candlestick," *Ariel*)

Little poppies, little hell flames

. . . .

. . . It exhausts me to watch you
Flickering like that, wrinkly and clear red, like the
skin of a mouth.
A mouth just bloodied.
Little bloody skirts!

. . . .

If I could bleed, or sleep!—
If my mouth could marry a hurt like that!
("Poppies in July," *Ariel*)

. . . the woman in the ambulance
Whose red heart blooms through her coat so astoundingly—
("Poppies in October," *Ariel*)

two children, two roses
("Kindness," *Ariel*)

Death: purity, emptiness, colorlessness, virginity, stars, moon, snow, perfection.

The tulips are too excitable, it is winter here.
Look how white everything is, how quiet, how snowed-in.

. . . .

I am a nun now, I have never been so pure.

I didn't want any flowers, I only wanted
To lie with my hands turned up and be utterly empty.
("Tulips," *Ariel*)

I do not stir.
The frost makes a flower,

The dew makes a star,
The dead bell,
The dead bell.

Somebody's done for.
("Death & Co.," *Ariel*)

. . . the cold dead center
where spilt lives congeal and stiffen to history.
("A Birthday Present," *Ariel*)

I am too pure for you or anyone.
Your body
Hurts me as the world hurts God. I am a lantern—

My head a moon ·
Of Japanese paper, my gold beaten skin
Infinitely delicate and infinitely expensive.
("Fever 103°," *Ariel*)

Perfection is terrible, it cannot have children.
Cold as snow breath, it tamps the womb

Where the yew trees blow like hydras,
The tree of life and the tree of life

Unloosing their moons, month after month, to no purpose.
The blood flood is the flood of love,

The absolute sacrifice.
("The Munich Mannequins," *Ariel*)

I saw death in the bare trees, a deprivation.
(*Three Women, Winter Trees*)

The moon is no door. It is a face in its own right,
White as a knuckle and terribly upset.
It drags the sea after it like a dark crime; it is quiet
With the O-gape of complete despair. I live here.
("The Moon and the Yew Tree," *Ariel*)

The woman is perfected.
Her dead

Body wears the smile of accomplishment,
The illusion of a Greek necessity

> Flows in the scrolls of her toga. . . .
> . . . .
> The moon has nothing to be sad about,
> Staring from her hood of bone.
> ("Edge," *Ariel*)

Yet the war between death and life is an ongoing process, and the poems as they evolve arrange and rearrange the symbols for elements of the poet's experience. These arrangements indicate the progress, the direction of the struggle itself.

In "Tulips," written in 1961, Plath describes herself as a hospital patient, recovering from an appendectomy. In this poem, the desire for death is overcome by the force of life. In long lines of narrative, the poem sets up a series of external correspondences to the poet's psychological state. Through her very perception of these "correspondences" as they actively exist and interact, the poet undergoes a gradual change in her condition.

She is "nobody": she has "let things slip, a thirty-year-old cargo boat"; she is "swabbed clear of her loving associations," "a nun," who has "never been so pure." She perceives the hospital and all associated with it as agents that assist in her quest for nonbeing: "I have given my name and my day-clothes up to the nurses / And my history to the anaesthetist and my body to the surgeons."

> . . . it is winter here.
> I am learning peacefulness, lying by myself quietly
> As the light lies on these white walls, this bed, these hands.

If the season of hospitals is winter, its element is water. The nurses are gulls:

> The nurses pass and pass, they are no trouble,
> They pass the way gulls pass inland in their white caps,
> Doing things with their hands, one just the same as another,
> So it is impossible to tell how many there are.

Her body is a pebble to them: "they tend it as water / Tends to the pebbles it must run over, smoothing them gently." Their bright needles bring her numbness, sleep. The gull/nurses have "swabbed her clean of her loving associations":

> Scared and bare on the green plastic-pillowed trolley
> I watched my tea-set, my bureaus of linen, my books
> Sink out of sight, and the water went over my head.

She wants the freedom, the peace that she identifies with the gift of death.

> How free it is, you have no idea how free—
> The peacefulness is so big it dazes you,
> And it asks nothing, a name tag, a few trinkets.
> It is what the dead close on, finally: I imagine them
> Shutting their mouths on it, like a Communion tablet.

But there is an alien presence in this wintry mindscape. The poem opens with it: "The tulips are too excitable." While the first five stanzas commemorate the force and fascination of death, culminating in the vision of the dead shutting their mouths on its great freedom and peacefulness like a Communion tablet, the irritant, the presence of the tulips, continues to bother and is perhaps the cause of such an extended paean to nonbeing. In the first stanza, the poet argues: "I am nobody; I have nothing to do with explosions." Again, she begins the fifth stanza, which ends with the reference to the Communion tablet, arguing: "I didn't want any flowers, I only wanted / To lie with my hands turned up and be utterly empty."

But the tulips cannot be ignored. They are "too red"; they watch, they breathe, they move. Their redness hurts: it "talks to my wound, it corresponds." They breathe "like an awful baby." They weigh her down, although they seem to float:

> Upsetting me with their sudden tongues and their colour,
> A dozen red lead sinkers around my neck.

And they watch; they turn to her, and make her see herself:

> . . . flat, ridiculous, a cut-paper shadow
> Between the eye of the sun and the eyes of the tulips,
> And I have no face, I have wanted to efface myself.
> The vivid tulips eat my oxygen.

The two stanzas of describing the tulips, of analyzing why she resents their presence, are already enough to cause her to notice a sun outside, to see herself in a new light, to begin to want to breathe the oxygen that the tulips are "eating." The tulips "correspond" to her wound, because like them she is alive, and their living presence forces her living response.

The concluding two stanzas are vivid with color and noise, as life, once acknowledged, seems to explode around the poet:

> Now the air snags and eddies round them the way a river
> Snags and eddies round a sunken rust-red engine.
> They concentrate my attention, that was happy
> Playing and resting without committing itself.

The icy sea has become a turbulent river, and the poet is caught up in it. For the season is changing: "the walls, also, seem to be warming themselves." The final correspondence is at last made: there is no escaping it. Even as the tulips open "like the mouth of some great African cat," so she becomes aware of her heart:

> . . . it opens and closes
> Its bowl of red blooms out of sheer love of me.
> The water I taste is warm and salt, like the sea,
> And comes from a country far away as health.

As the tulips become a fierce, warm-blooded African cat, so her own heart becomes a bowl of flowers, the tulips themselves. Her heart equals flowers and flowers equal animals because all are alive, full of color, full of motion. So, too, is the sea, once the ice has melted from its surface (from all the heat, the warmth of breath and blood), and it too can flow freely.

It is Plath's method to express her ideas in terms of such "correspondences": the quality of her vision (here, one that sees gulls and pebbles, babies and African cats) has always set in motion the symbolic action of her poems. What is different now is that the person having that vision is a part of it and affected by it: what and how the poet "sees" affects what happens to her in the poem, even as what happens to her as the main character in the poem affects what and how she sees. In this instance, the positive power of life (flowers, babies, redness, breath) overwhelms the negative pull of death (whiteness, winter, ice, snow, passivity, purity, emptiness, peacefulness, freedom); and the action of the poem is the battle that is waged. The detached and distant observer is no more.

In the last poems the love between mother and child is described again and again. It appears as the strongest agent for life, having the most powerful hold upon the poet. In Plath's longest poem, *Three Women*, three women in a maternity ward speak of their experience of motherhood. The first voice is that of a woman committed to maternity and nothing else. She is linked to the physical world: "I am slow as the world"; "I am breaking apart like the world"; "I am a river of milk. / I am a warm hill." The second voice is that of a woman who has had a series of miscarriages: she cannot conceive. She equates her condition with death and masculinity.

> When I first saw it, the small red seep, I did not believe it.
> I watched the men walk about me in the office. They were so flat!
> There was something.about them like cardboard, and now I had caught it,
> That flat, flat, flatness from which ideas, destructions,
> Bulldozers, guillotines, white chambers of shrieks proceed,
> Endlessly proceed—and the cold angels, the abstractions.
> . . . .
> This is a disease I carry home, this is a death.
> Again, this is a death. Is it the air,
> The particles of destruction I suck up? Am I a pulse
> That wanes and wanes, facing the cold angel?
> Is this my lover then? This death, this death?
> . . . .
> I shall move north. I shall move into a long blackness.
> I see myself as a shadow, neither man nor woman,
> Neither a woman, happy to be like a man, nor a man
> Blunt and flat enough to feel no lack. I feel a lack.
> I hold my fingers up, ten white pickets.
> See, the darkness is leaking from the cracks.
> I cannot contain it. I cannot contain my life.

The third voice is that of a college student who is having an illegitimate child that she does not keep. She equates her child with danger for her freedom, for her seriousness. She speaks of her "red, terrible girl," whose cries are "hooks that catch and grate like cats," whose cries are "Scratching at my sleep like arrows, / Scratching at my sleep and entering my side." Near the close of the poem, when she has returned to the university, she says:

> The books I carry wedge into my side.
> I had an old wound once, but it is healing.
> I had a dream of an island, red with cries.
> It was a dream, and did not mean a thing,

She praises her lack of attachments, her aloneness.

> Hot noon in the meadows. The buttercups
> Swelter and melt, and the lovers
> Pass by, pass by.
> They are black and flat as shadows.
> It is so beautiful to have no attachments!
> I am solitary as grass. What is it that I miss?
> Shall I ever find it, whatever it is?
>
> . . . .
>
> What is that bird that cries
> With such sorrow in its voice?
> I am young as ever, it says. What is it that I miss?

She has underestimated the power of maternity, of the love that she has given up. Some feminists have attacked *Three Women* because it is virtually a hymn to motherhood, to the woman's body as a physical instrument. Yet surely the poem must be viewed in the context of Plath's art, and life, as the expression of a yearning for a simple commitment that it is impossible for her to make, no matter how fiercely she feels its call and gifts. In maternity and in maternal love, the elements that Plath has always associated with life—pain, cries, breath, redness, blood, love, and babies—come together. Yet, as symbols for life, the mother and child are as impermanent, as fluid as the elements of which they are composed. Love is not enough to fix them; the perfect child will leave the mother, will enter the world, will know death: "O golden child the world will kill and eat" ("Mary's Song").

> *Child*
>
> Your clear eye is the one absolutely beautiful thing.
> I want to fill it with color and ducks,
> The zoo of the new
>
> Whose names you meditate—
> April snowdrop, Indian pipe,
> Little

Stalk without wrinkle,
Pool in which images
Should be grand and classical

Not this troublous
Wringing of hands, this dark
Ceiling without a star.

(*Winter Trees*)

One cannot find one's own perfection through another human being, even one's own child. This is the lesson that Plath learns from trying to do it. Forever seeking perfection, first in herself (but finding it to be a lie, a farce, an illusion), she then seeks it in her children: "Your clear eye is the one absolutely beautiful thing." She wants to fill the child's eye, as a poem, with the beauty and good of the world as she sees it; she wants it to be a mirror, reflecting back the images of perfection that she cannot make in herself: "Pool in which images / Should be grand and classical." But there is no help for it: the child's eye reflects herself, reflects the world: "this troublous / Wringing of hands, this dark / Ceiling without a star." If one seeks perfection, as Plath did, there is finally only one source left: death.

"Edge" (*Ariel*) was written during the last week of Plath's life. It is as spare and terse as "Tulips" was narrative and conversational. It is nothing but vision: a vision of herself, now, no longer operating in any external world. Elements from the physical world are useful, valid, real, only as they help her to define with words her own consciousness. She has come to see with an awful clarity that the only reality is what she makes. She did not make herself. She made her children and her poems; and she can make her death. In her poem, she makes that death with words.

The woman is perfected.
Her dead

Body wears the smile of accomplishment,
The illusion of a Greek necessity

Flows in the scrolls of her toga,
Her bare

Feet seem to be saying:
We have come so far, it is over.

Perfection, accomplishment, death—these ideas are embodied in the corpse of a woman with "the illusion of a Greek necessity" flowing in the "scrolls" of her toga. The very folds of her clothing are in exactly the right position, as if fated to be there; everything about her form is correct, exact, the fulfillment of her destiny. So I paraphrase Plath's figure of speech, but the form in which she expressed this thought is itself significant: the way in which the concepts "illusion" and "necessity" take action (flow) and physical shape in the scrolls of a toga represents the merging of concept and object that is the subject of the poem.

This woman is a mother; but here the problem of losing the child to the world has been solved, for the children, too, are dead:

> Each dead child coiled, a white serpent
> One at each little
>
> Pitcher of milk, now empty.

In this poem, the opposition between images and symbols—red versus white, blood versus ice—that occurs in so many of her works has been reconciled, or surmounted. Dead, a child is white.

> She has folded
>
> Them back into her body as petals
> Of a rose close when the garden
>
> Stiffens and odours bleed
> From the sweet, deep throats of the night flower.

Children, flowers, and blood still go together, but it has been understood here that flowers also die, that the blood that pulses through the veins and symbolizes life is the same blood that flows out to create death. Returned to their original unity with the mother, the children have therefore recaptured their prelapsarian perfection.

> The moon has nothing to be sad about,
> Staring from her hood of bone.
>
> She is used to this sort of thing.
> Her blacks crackle and drag.

The moon, as in many Plath poems, remains the proper light, and audience, for a death scene: her cold and carved whiteness reflects and illuminates the cold corpse with its sculptured form. The woman has become her own tombstone, her own monument.

In his study of suicide, *The Savage God*,[19] Alvarez argues quite convincingly that in her last suicide attempt, as in all of her former attempts, Plath did not really mean to die and tried to make it possible for someone to save her; but that a series of unfortunate coincidences prevented that salvation from occurring. He may well be correct: many people attempt suicide as an ultimate gesture, the most extreme and the strongest that they know, that says in effect: Help me! Pay attention to me! I cannot handle things alone! I need help! Surely the social and physical conditions that Plath was experiencing in her last months—a bitter winter, frozen pipes, no telephone, unpredictable heat and electricity, no help with the children, separation from her husband, her own illness—were the mitigating circumstances that caused intense depression, a feeling that she could no longer go it alone and needed help. She did not have to die in the winter of 1963. But it seems inevitable that at some point she would have caused her own death. Its attractions were so very great for her, because there was, finally, no solution to her life. She is the woman poet of our century who sees the problem, the situation of trying to be a woman poet with the coldest and most unredeeming clarity, and who, try as she might, finds no solution. Being the best poet, being the best mother, will not solve the problem, because there remains the yawning gap between poet and mother, her sense of herself as not one but two.

Her death, because it is no solution, proves the impossibility of what she set out to do, which may be why she has been such a satisfying idol for both those who do not believe that women have a right to be both women and poets and those who believe in the right, but as an ideal that can never be achieved in the practical world. Surely she was a victim of her situation, yet others before and since in a similar position have not responded exactly as she did, either because they did not perceive it as she did or because they found other ways out of it. Ultimately, we cannot distinguish between her situation, herself, and her art. She would not have killed herself if she had not been in that particular position and had not perceived it as she did, but neither would she have been the woman she was, the poet she was, if she had not lived and written under those conditions.

Yet her death was in every sense tragic because it was *not* necessary;

because the social and psychological pressures that led her to it need not have existed—need not exist. When I read Plath's poetry, I am frightened by it, but I am not led, as she was, through it towards death. It makes me want more than ever to be allowed to live; to fight in whatever ways I can find to be able to live as both woman and poet; to make it possible for these to be harmonious facets of one person. Because Plath lived, and died, and wrote as she did, this goal has become more possible. Her courage to work from the reality that she knew can be emulated; her defeat in the face of that reality can be a lesson to avoid.

NOTES

1. Erica Jong, *Fruits and Vegetables* (New York: Holt, Rinehart and Winston, 1971), p. 47.
2. Robert Lowell, Foreword to *Ariel* (New York: Harper and Row, 1965), p. viii.
3. Charles Newman, "Candor is the Only Wile: The Art of Sylvia Plath," in Charles Newman, ed., *The Art of Sylvia Plath: A Symposium* (Bloomington and London: Indiana University Press, 1971), p. 27.
4. M. L. Rosenthal, "Sylvia Plath and Confessional Poetry," in Newman, ed., *The Art of Sylvia Plath: A Symposium*, p. 71.
5. As documented by Lois Ames in "Notes Toward a Biography," in Newman, ed., *The Art of Sylvia Plath: A Symposium*, pp. 160–61.
6. *The Bell Jar* (New York: Bantam Books, 1972), p. 62.
7. Ibid., pp. 104–5.
8. Ames, "Notes Towards a Biography," in Newman, ed., *The Art of Sylvia Plath: A Symposium*, p. 160.
9. *The Colossus And Other Poems* (New York: Vintage Books, 1968).
10. Ted Hughes, "Notes on the Chronological Order of Sylvia Plath's Poems," in Newman, ed., *The Art of Sylvia Plath: A Symposium*, p. 188.
11. A. Alvarez, "Sylvia Plath," in Newman, ed., *The Art of Sylvia Plath: A Symposium*, p. 58.
12. Charles Newman, "Candor is the Only Wile: The Art of Sylvia Plath," in Newman, ed., *The Art of Sylvia Plath: A Symposium*, p. 46.
13. Alvarez, "Sylvia Plath," in Newman, ed., *The Art of Sylvia Plath: A Symposium*, p. 58.
14. *Ariel*, p. 4.
15. *Crossing the Water* (New York: Harper and Row, 1971), pp. 30–33.

16. Hughes, "Notes on the Chronological Order of Sylvia Plath's Poems," in Newman, ed., *The Art of Sylvia Plath: A Symposium*, p. 187.
17. Quoted by Alvarez, "Sylvia Plath," in Newman, ed., *The Art of Sylvia Plath: A Symposium*, p. 59.
18. *Winter Trees* (New York: Harper and Row, 1972).
19. A. Alvarez, *The Savage God* (London: Weidenfeld and Nicolson, 1971), pp. 5–34.

6

"The Excitable Gift": The Poetry of Anne Sexton

This study of Anne Sexton's poetry was written before her death in October 1974. In it I describe her growing power through poetry, a triumph of life over death. Now it is apparent that the lure of death—always present, as her poems attest—grew too strong for her, despite the poetry. Yet her death does not negate either her art or the strength that she achieved through it. For the years in which she wrote, she held death at bay and with her poems sent a powerful awareness of life into the world. It was her tragedy, like that of others before her, to be both woman and poet. The struggle in this double-bind situation between such conflicting role demands is excrutiating for all who will not choose between being "woman" or "poet." Anne Sexton's poetry is a testament to her courage and ability to be both for as long as she could.

"To rage in your own bowl"

Anne Sexton came to poetry through psychotherapy. She became a poet after having experienced the traditional woman's roles of wife, mother, housewife; *because* she had experienced them and needed a way, a form, a voice with which to deal with the fact of being a woman.

"Until I was twenty-eight I had a kind of buried self who didn't know she could do anything but make white sauce and diaper babies," she remarked in 1968 to a *Paris Review* interviewer:

> All I wanted was a little piece of life, to be married, to have children. I thought the nightmares, the visions, would go away if there was enough love to put them down. I was trying my damnedest to lead a conventional life, for that was how I was brought up, and it was what my husband wanted of me. But one can't build little white picket fences to keep the nightmares out. The surface cracked when I was about twenty-eight. I had a psychotic break and tried to kill myself.[1]

After she began to write poems, her therapist encouraged her: " 'Don't kill yourself,' he said. 'Your poems might mean something to someone else someday.' That gave me a feeling of purpose, a little cause, something to *do* with my life, no matter how rotten I was."[2]

Since Betty Friedan first analyzed "the problem that has no name,"[3] psychologists, sociologists, and others writing about women have described the kind of situation in which Sexton found herself and have provided extensive insight into the sources of the kind of madness that she experienced. In discussing the poetry that she created, it is essential to observe that her "confessionalism" grew out of the therapy situation, but that the therapy was occasioned by her womanhood itself, by the very real strains and conflicts that Sexton experienced while attempting to exist in her world as a woman.

The poems from *To Bedlam and Part Way Back* (1960)[4] to the volume appropriately titled *Live or Die* (1966)[5] closely follow the psychoanalytic model. They move in concern from the present or near past, from the trappings of madness (its hospitals, inmates, doctors, pills) to the more distant past in which the madness grew. It is a past not so much of events as relationships—relations with blood kin: mother, father, daughters. Endlessly exploring herself as she has been created by these interpersonal relationships, Sexton probes for the truth. The way back to sanity is through understanding, yet we may understand better with the unconscious than with the conscious mind. As artist, Sexton wills the memories with her conscious mind (sometimes, as in "All My Pretty Ones," "Walking in Paris," "Some Foreign Letters," photographs or letters are carefully used as occasions to awaken memory), but the unconscious mind, it is hoped, will supply the images, the connections and associations that will give access to the truth. "The poetry is often more advanced, in terms of my unconscious, than I am," she tells the interviewer. "Poetry, after all, milks the unconscious. The unconscious is there to feed it little images, little symbols, the answers, the insights I know not of."[6] Thus in her poems she describes herself as patient: "And I am queen of this summer hotel / or the laughing bee on a stalk / of death" ("You, Doctor Martin");[7] her mother: "That was the winter / that my mother died, / half mad on morphine, / blown up, at last, / like a pregnant pig. / I was her dreamy evil eye" ("Flee On Your Donkey");[8] her daughter: ". . . I just pretended / you, small piglet, butterfly / girl with jelly bean cheeks" ("The Double Image").[9]

The most characteristic form for these images is the simile or epithet-metaphor: "Words are like labels, / or coins, or better, like swarming bees," she writes in "Said the Poet to the Analyst."[10] The following litany to her dead mother is based upon her understanding (consistent with psychoanalytic theory) of the power of naming itself to define and to exorcise.

> Now it is Friday's noon
> and I would still curse
> you with my rhyming words
> and bring you flapping back, old love,
> old circus knitting, god-in-her-moon,
> all fairest in my lang syne verse,
> The gauzy bride among the children,
> the fancy amid the absurd
> and awkward, that horn for hounds
> that skipper homeward, that museum
> keeper of stiff starfish, that blaze
> within the pilgrim woman,
> a clown mender, a dove's
> cheek among the stones,
> my Lady of my first words,
> this is the division of ways.
>
> ("The Division of Parts")[11]

First the naming, difficult enough; then, frequently, the definition expanded into a complex image: "I must always forget how one word is able to pick / out another, to manner another, until I have got / something I might have said" ("Said the Poet to the Analyst"). Thus Sexton "sees" her maternal guilt this way:

> . . . Ugly angels spoke to me. The blame,
> I heard them say, was mine. They tattled
> like green witches in my head, letting doom
> leak like a broken faucet;
> as if doom had flooded my belly and filled your bassinet,
> an old debt I must assume.
>
> ("The Double Image")

"The Double Image," a long poem in eight sections from *To Bedlam and Part Way Back*, offers a good example of the method by which Anne Sexton in her early poetry analyzes the nature of her madness and her identity in terms of personal relationships: here, with her mother and her daughter. The poem begins in the present tense: mother and daughter stand by a window in November, watching the leaves fall. Yet this mother and child have been parted for three years because of the mother's madness and attempted suicide; the physical fact of their reunion is the result of a series of psychological facts, and events, which the poet, explaining to her daughter, explores by going back in time and memory. When the child, Joyce, asks where the yellow leaves go, her mother answers rather cryptically, that "today believed / in itself, or else it fell." She continues:

> Today, my small child, Joyce,
> love your self's self where it lives.
> There is no special God to refer to; or if there is,
> why did I let you grow
> in another place.
>
> (Part 1)

She then offers, in six poems, her memories to explain this advice.

Briefly, she describes her first suicide attempt (directly resulting from her guilt over the child's first serious illness) and the mental hospital. Then she focuses on the years when she was "part way back from Bedlam," living with her mother ("Too late, / too late, to live with your mother, the witches said") while her child lived elsewhere, occasionally visiting. The poem moves in anguish back and forth between the partial, inadequate relationship between the poet and her mother—

I cannot forgive your suicide, my mother said.
And she never could. She had my portrait
done instead.

(Part 2)

Only my mother grew ill.
She turned from me, as if death were catching,
as if death transferred,
as if my dying had eaten inside of her.
That August you were two, but I timed my days with doubt.
On the first of September she looked at me
and said I gave her cancer.
They carved her sweet hills out
and still I couldn't answer.

(Part 3)

—and the partial, inadequate relationship between the poet and her daughter:

Once I mailed you a picture of a rabbit
and a postcard of Motif number one,
as if it were normal
to be a mother and be gone.

(Part 3)

I could not get you back
except for weekends. You came
each time, clutching the picture of a rabbit
that I had sent you . . .

The first visit you asked my name.
. . . I will forget
how we bumped away from each other like marionettes
on strings. It wasn't the same
as love, letting weekends contain
us.

(Part 7)

The fragmented nature of these relationships is poised against the poet's constant recognition of a profound underlying identity between herself and her mother, herself and her daughter: "Your smile is like your mother's, the artist said" (Part 2).

> During the sea blizzards
> she had her
> own portrait painted.
> A cave of a mirror
> placed on the south wall;
> matching smile, matching contour.
> And you resembled me; unacquainted
> with my face, you wore it. But you were mine
> after all.
>
> (Part 4)

The poet is caught between two images of herself that reflect her to herself, but each only partially; because as reflections they rely on her for their identity as much as she relies on them. And she has no sense of herself, of who she is, only guilt for the kind of daughter and mother she thinks she might be.

To talk about a condition of simultaneous separation and identity, the poem projects a series of "double images." The central double image is the pair of portraits, mother and daughter, in "the house that waits / still, on top of the sea," where "two portraits hang on opposite walls" (Part 5). Yet mirrors, windows, and people themselves also reflect the idea, as the poem's words describe the portraits:

> In south light, her smile is held in place,
> her cheeks wilting like a dry
> orchid; my mocking mirror, my overthrown
> love, my first image. She eyes me from that face,
> that stony head of death
> I had outgrown . . .
>
> And this was the cave of the mirror,
> that double woman who stares
> at herself, as if she were petrified
> in time—two ladies sitting in umber chairs.
> You kissed your grandmother
> and she cried.
>
> (Part 6)

Analyzing those years of the portraits in Part 5, the poet is, I think, also describing the movement of her poem:

> . . . And I had to learn
> why I would rather
> die than love, how your innocence
> would hurt and how I gather
> guilt like a young intern
> his symptoms, his certain evidence.
> (Part 5)

Part 7, the poem's final section, returns to the present tense of Part 1: "Now you stay for good / . . . You call me *mother* and I remember my mother again, / somewhere in greater Boston, dying." It returns to mother and daughter at the window, looking out on the world, another double image. Yet the poem ends with a final memory, the mother's memory of her child as an infant, "all wrapped and moist / and strange at my heavy breast. / I needed you," in order that the poet may offer her understanding of herself to her daughter:

> I, who was never quite sure
> about being a girl, needed another
> life, another image to remind me.
> And this was my worst guilt; you could not cure
> nor soothe it. I made you to find me.
> (Part 7)

The initial realization of her connection with her daughter had led the poet *into* madness: "as if doom had flooded my belly and filled your bassinet, / an old debt I must assume" (Part 1); now an understanding of the same connection has led her out of madness. The difference, predictable in psychoanalytic terms, lies not in any severing of the connection, but in a dissolution of the guilt that arose from it. "I made you to find me," says the poet. And why not, because surely in some ways I am you and you are me, a girl child that I have made in my woman's body; and in other ways you are not me, I am not you, for I am mother, while you are child. We are a double image.

The ending and beginning of the poem focus upon the poet and her daughter, because this relationship, although dependent for its very being upon that other double image, the poet-daughter and *her* mother, can lead into life, while the other one cannot. This is not only because the poet's mother is literally dying, but because the guilt involved with that relationship is not gone. Whatever understanding has been achieved is partial and has come too late: "Too late to be forgiven now, the witches said" (Part 2). The mother had accused her daughter of causing her death, and the poet could not answer, feeling the truth of the accusation, and feeling guilty for it.

The poem has demonstrated what the poet meant when in Part 1 she advised loving oneself's self where it lives. True relationships between people, any kind of relationships, but especially those between people of blood ties, where a profound connection or identity exists, cannot occur unless each member of the pair is secure in her own identity. Granted that that identity may depend upon and even arise out of the relationship, it must yet be distinct: the person cannot *confuse* herself with the other person in the relationship. The double image can be both positive and negative, as it is in this poem: negative when it reflects beings who are creating their identities out of the reflections that they see, that in turn are creating identities out of the reflections that they see, that in turn, and on and on, into infinity; positive when each watcher sees another person who is like herself, who reflects herself, but who also reflects her own self!

If, as "The Double Image" and many of her early poems reveal, the cause of Sexton's madness and its accompanying desire for death has been her woman's situation, experience, identity, it is also true that the affirmation of life at which she arrives through the acts of her poems is founded in her womanhood. "Live," the final poem in her third book, *Live or Die*, helps her to locate the source of and reason for life in woman's situation, experience, identity.

> Today life opened inside me like an egg
> and there inside
> after considerable digging
> I found the answer.
> What a bargain!
> There was the sun,
> her yolk moving feverishly,
> tumbling her prize—
> and you realize that she does this daily!
> I'd known she was a purifier
> but I hadn't thought

she was solid,
hadn't known she was an answer.
("Live")

Life, of course, comes from inside herself—spiritually as well as physically. It is an egg, is life; and an egg is the sun, for the sun is an egg, for the sun is life; and it is not outside herself at all, for her to bask or not to bask in its (reflected) light. No, it is *inside* herself, and it is she who must deliver it, give it birth, make life happen. It is she who makes the world; it is an extension of her very body. "So I say *Live* / and turn my shadow three times round":

So I won't hang around in my hospital shift,
repeating the Black Mass and all of it.
I say *Live, Live* because of the sun,
the dream, the excitable gift.

Being a poet causes Anne Sexton to understand herself as possessor of "the excitable gift," because the act of poetry unites understanding with experience; its vision is insight. Though her poetry begins as therapy for her personal salvation, because it is a public act it reaches out to others. Yet it is always rooted in her personal self, her private life, as is the sun. It does not, like much of the "confessional" poetry of men, abstract or generalize upon its own experiences, either explicitly or implicitly; nevertheless, it communicates to others and offers its gift. In an early poem, "For John, Who Begs Me Not to Enquire Further" (*To Bedlam and Part Way Back*),[12] Sexton herself tries to explain how this gift works. Commenting upon her explorations of self, of "that narrow diary of my mind," she finds their purpose to have been, not beauty, but "a certain sense of order there." If she had tried "to give [him] something else, / something outside of myself," he would not then know "that the worst of anyone / can be, finally, / an accident of hope." Generalizing, in other words, destroys the very meaning sought.

I tapped my own head;
it was glass, an inverted bowl.
It is a small thing
To rage in your own bowl.
At first it was private.
Then it was more than myself;
it was you, or your house

or your kitchen.
And if you turn away
because there is no lesson here
I will hold my awkward bowl,
with all its cracked stars shining
like a complicated lie,
and fasten a new skin around it
as if I were dressing an orange
or a strange sun.
Not that it was beautiful,
but that I found some order there.
There ought to be something special
for someone
in this kind of hope.

("For John, Who Begs Me Not to Enquire Further")

"A middle-aged witch, me"

Love Poems (1969),[13] the volume that follows *Live or Die,* is a further extension of the decision for life into the living experience of love; it is almost a postscript to the previous volume. It is with the next book of poems, *Transformations* (1971),[14] that a major development, if not a transformation, does in fact begin to occur. Here Sexton shows where her journey from patient to poet has led her. It has led her to understand the positive potential of herself as "middle-aged witch, me." Previous to this volume, she has equated madwoman and witch: "I have gone out, a possessed witch, / haunting the black air, braver at night" ("Her Kind," *To Bedlam and Part Way Back*). The refrain of "Her Kind" develops as follows: "A woman like that is not a woman, quite. / I have been her kind"; "A woman like that is misunderstood. / I have been her kind"; "A woman like that is not ashamed to die. / I have been her kind." The green witches of "The Double Image" who spoke inside Sexton's head of truth asked for death in payment for insight. Madness must lead to death, because the mad are "magic talking to itself, / noisy and alone" ("You, Doctor Martin"). "Talking" is a key word here, and equally so is "alone." Nobody listens; the language of the mad, like the world of women, is private. Nobody (the world) *cares* to hear, to know; for the world would not like what it learned. Yet if no one listens, the voice destroys itself with its truths. As has often been pointed out, the distance between fool or madman and poet is not great. Nor is the space between madwoman and woman poet, but it is less frequently traversed. Madwomen are doubly relegated to the private world, as mad and as women, while "poet" traditionally belongs to the male, the public world. The voice of the poet is a public voice; the poet's words affect other people: they may even cause changes, action. It is a voice of power. As Sexton's analyst had told her, poems can mean something to someone. For Sexton, as woman, the move from patient to poet has been a voyage from dependence and powerlessness to independence and power. By rooting her public voice in her private experience, by creating a public persona, witch, out of her private self, witch, she is able to discuss the race in addition to herself. The witch is a wisewoman, storyteller, seer. A witch works magic: her magic is and has always been the magic of words, so that the word "magic" in the line from "You, Doctor Martin" is also a key word. Thus it is fitting that Sexton's poetic language itself, from *Transformations* on, embodies and expresses this development.

Her power as poet arises from the power, the magic of words: the witch/poet's spells make things happen; they plant "words in you like grass seed" ("Iron Hans").[15] In her early poetry, Sexton, as madwoman and potential suicide (only "part way back"), had to control her images, her metaphors and similes of association, by the conscious forms of meter, rhyme, and the sentence itself, which consistently supplied the links between images of insight. In *Transformations* Sexton begins to abandon a great deal of this "control," because, I think, she feels in control. Now bold figures of association cast their spell with little to mediate their effect.

In *Transformations* Sexton begins to extend her original themes. In later volumes, *The Book of Folly*[16] and *The Death Notebooks*,[17] she will make her own myths. Here, she is warming up on Grimm's scales. She retells *Grimm's Fairy Tales*, with "the speaker in this case / . . . a middle-aged witch, me." These tales do for the history of the race what the earlier poems did for Sexton's personal history: they attempt to create the truth by bridging the gap between the present of adult experience, the potential madness underlying the everyday, and the past of childhood, dream, and archetype. Like the earlier poetry, these poems move from present to past (the therapy situation), not from the traditional once-upon-a-time to the moral that encompasses the present and all future time. They begin with present-day examples of situations of which the tales are archetypes, and Dame Sexton feels no compunction against using herself as a present-day example.

> If you danced from midnight
> to six A.M. who would understand? . . .
>
> The night nurse
> with her eyes slit like Venetian blinds,
> she of the tubes and the plasma,
> listening to the heart monitor,
> the death cricket bleeping,
> she who calls you "we"
> and keeps vigil like a ballistic missile,
> would understand.
> ("The Twelve Dancing Princesses")
>
> Many are the deceivers: . . .
>
> And I. I too.
> Quite collected at cocktail parties,
> meanwhile in my head
> I'm undergoing open-heart surgery.
> The heart, poor fellow,
> pounding on his little tin drum
> with a faint death beat.
> The heart, that eyeless beetle,
> enormous Kafka beetle,
> running panicked through his maze,
> never stopping one foot after the other
> one hour after the other
> until he gags on an apple
> and it's all over.
> ("Red Riding Hood")

Here Sexton's characteristic figures of association are especially bold: the juxtaposition of seemingly incongruous material that, upon contact, produces sparks, shocks of definition, revelation—"her eyes slit like Venetian blinds"; "keeps vigil like a ballistic missile"; "The heart, that eyeless beetle, / enormous Kafka beetle." The similes and epithet-metaphors embedded in the "fairy" part of the tales are particularly interesting, as they enact in microcosm the present to past movement of the poems: "tenor" belongs to the tale, the past, while "vehicle" belongs to the present, specifically modern situation—"[Rumpelstiltskin] tore himself in two. / Somewhat like a split broiler"; "The King looked like Munch's *Scream*"; "at the wedding the princesses averted their eyes / and sagged like old sweatshirts."

The tales that Dame Sexton chooses from Grimm's collection deal with her favorite themes: madness, death, and women. A cluster of the stories, "Snow White and the Seven Dwarfs," "The White Snake," "The Little Peasant," "Rapunzel," "Cinderella," "Red Riding Hood," "The Twelve Dancing Princesses," and "Briar Rose (Sleeping Beauty)," project without idealism the possible roles for women in the world. Young girls, heroines and princesses, begin in a state of mindless natural beauty, in an innocence and purity that is defined by its total physicality: "a daughter as lovely as a grape . . . / Poor grape with no one to pick. / Luscious and round and sleek" ("Rumpelstiltskin"); "The princess was as ripe as a tangerine. / Her breasts purred up and down like a cat" ("Godfather Death"):

> No matter what life you lead
> the virgin is a lovely number:
> cheeks as fragile as cigarette paper,
> arms and legs made of Limoges,
> lips like Vin Du Rhône,
> rolling her china-blue doll eyes
> open and shut.
> Open to say,
> Good Day Mama,
> and shut for the thrust
> of the unicorn.
> She is unsoiled.
> She is as white as a bonefish.
> ("Snow White and the Seven Dwarfs")

They move to the inevitable corruption of sexuality—"They lay together upon the yellowy threads [Rapunzel's hair], / swimming through them / like minnows through kelp / and they sang out benedictions like the Pope" ("Rapunzel")—and thence to either meaninglessness or madness (or both).

> Meanwhile Snow White held court,
> rolling her china-blue doll eyes open and shut
> and sometimes referring to her mirror
> as women do.
> ("Snow White and the Seven Dwarfs")

> Briar Rose
> was an insomniac . . .

> Each night I am nailed into place
> and I forget who I am.
> Daddy?
> That's another kind of prison.
> It's not the prince at all, .
> but my father
> drunkenly bent over my bed,
> circling the abyss like a shark,
> my father thick upon me
> like some sleeping jellyfish.
> ("Briar Rose")

Like proper fairy tales, these abound with witches, for the witch has been traditionally the figure of the woman past middle age. Many of these women are embittered ex-princesses, like the wicked stepmother of "Snow White," "a beauty in her own right, / though eaten, of course, by age," or embittered spinsters, like the thirteenth fairy of "Briar Rose," "her fingers as long and thin as straws, / her eyes burnt by cigarettes, / her uterus as empty as a teacup." Primarily, their power is for evil, evil to aid in the corruption of innocence, corrupting the young into their own state of bitter age. Only Dame Sexton herself, because she is a poet, has broken the system and works for truth, if not goodness:

> And then I knew that the voice
> of the spirits had been let in—
> as intense as an epileptic aura—
> and that no longer would I sing
> alone.
> ("The White Snake")

There are no mothers and daughters in these tales, only daughters and lecherous fathers or evil stepmothers. Only once does Sexton attempt an analysis of a kind of mother-daughter relationship in the story of "Rapunzel," and here both the questions and the answers are fraught with ambiguity, as Sexton trods on dangerous ground in postulating any possible kind of salvation for women in the real world.

"Rapunzel" begins this way: "A woman / who loves a woman / is forever young." It is the tale of a witch, Mother Gothel, who had a magic garden, "more beautiful than Eve's." But this witch, unlike Eve, is a spinster. When a pregnant woman yearns for a magic root in her garden, the rampion, "a kind of harebell more potent than penicillin," the witch strikes a bargain, "typical enough in those times," with the woman's husband whom she catches in the garden: he promises his child to her. This is, of course, Rapunzel, "another name for the life-giving Rampion." The witch vows that none but she will ever see or touch the beautiful girl and locks her in a high tower. Together, the pseudo-mother and daughter "play mother-me-do / all day." The witch sings:

> Give me your nether lips
> all puffy with their art
> and I will give you angel fire in return.
> We are two clouds
> glistening in the bottle glass.
> We are two birds
> washing in the same mirror.
> We were fair game
> but we have kept out of the cesspool.
> We are strong.
> We are the good ones.
> Do not discover us
> for we lie together all in green
> like pond weeds.
> Hold me, my young dear, hold me.

But the prince comes, as he always seems to do. Rapunzel is startled at this "beast . . . / with muscles on his arms / like a bag of snakes," by the "moss on his legs," and the "prickly plant that grows on his cheeks."

> Yet he dazzled her with his answers.
> Yet he dazzled her with his dancing stick.

When the so-called happy ending has occurred, Sexton pronounces upon it this way:

> They lived happily as you might expect
> proving that mother-me-do
> can be outgrown,
> just as the fish on Friday,
> just as a tricycle.
> The world, some say,
> is made up of couples.
> A rose must have a stem.

As for Mother Gothel, her heart shrinks to the size of a pin, never again to say "Hold me, my young dear, / hold me, / and only as she dreamt of the yellow hair / did moonlight sift into her mouth."

These tales are insistent upon the uncompromising reality of the real world, a place where neither childhood (tricycles), nor ideals (the fish on Friday), nor fantasy (dreaming of yellow hair) have any place or power. The love of Mother Gothel for her "daughter" seems to belong to all three; and although the plot of the poem, of the fairy tale, allows her no recourse, the language of the poem seems to be holding out for some other kind of validity: the bag of snakes and the dancing stick are posed against the two birds washing in the same mirror, the two clouds glistening in the bottle glass. The prince seems like a figurative as well as a literal comedown for Rapunzel, the "cesspool" out of which lesbian love with Mother Gothel had been keeping her. The other tales support this interpretation, with their portrayals of the fate of princesses. After having read all their happy endings (Cinderella and her prince, for example, living "they say" happily ever after, "like two dolls in a museum case / . . . never telling the same story twice, / never getting a middle-aged spread, / their darling smiles pasted on for eternity. / Regular Bobbsey Twins"), one might prefer the moonlight of Mother Gothel's dreams. Yet the questions remain: Were Rapunzel and Mother Gothel "the good ones"? Ought mother-me-do to be outgrown?

"For we swallow magic and we deliver Anne"

The Book of Folly (1972) and *The Death Notebooks* (1974) are experimental, bold, frightening. The poet consorts with angels, Furies, Mary, Jesus, gods, and death in the writing of stories, poems, psalms. These works make it clear that she trusted her vision, wherever it might take her. The old themes are in no way gone, but their expression frequently occurs in a new dimension. It is difficult now to label this poetry "confessional," because the talking voice, immersing itself in memory and experience, is gone; the voice now chants or sings, and experience has been transformed into myth. Nevertheless, the poems still refuse to generalize, to abstract: the "awkward bowl" of Sexton's consciousness is more of a "strange sun" than ever: it is a dangerous and magical world of visionary truth-saying.

In her middle forties, Anne Sexton continued to be faithful to her own perceptions. Death became a major element in what she perceived: the death of age, the result of commitment to life. Two poems to her daughter Linda, at ages eleven and eighteen, about the coming of womanhood, document this change in tone. In "Little Girl, My String-bean, My Lovely Woman" (*Live or Die*), the poet says: "How can I say that I've known / just what you know and just where you are?"

> Oh darling, let your body in,
> let it tie you in,
> in comfort.
> What I want to say, Linda,
> is that women are born twice . . .
>
> What I want to say, Linda,
> is that there is nothing in your body that lies.
> All that is new is telling the truth.
> I'm here, that somebody else,
> an old tree in the background.

In "Mother and Daughter" (*The Book of Folly*), the mother is at another stage in the process of physical connection and identification with her daughter, even as the daughter is at another stage, now a woman grown:

> Linda, you are leaving
> your old body now.
> You've picked my pocket clean
> and you've racked up all my
> poker chips and left me empty . . .
>
> Question you about this
> and you will see my death
> drooling at these gray lips

while you, my burglar, will eat
fruits and pass the time of day.

"The Death Baby," a poem in six parts from *The Death Notebooks*, explores the nature of death in terms (now familiar) of woman's roles of daughter and mother. Death may be generalizable, and universal, since like birth it is an experience that all humans share; but one's own death is personal, private, peculiarly one's own. In this poem, Sexton is trying to know her death.

The poem is a process, perhaps of initiation: one knows death when one is ready, and when death is ready to be known. This process has six stages. In the first, the poet explores death in dreams; the "exploration" is not an analysis but a vision of dream death: her own death, as a baby, in the dreams of her older sister. The second is death by fantasy: the vision of a doll's death. The third is the lesson of death attempted, premature or false death: the vision, in the dream of the would-be suicide, is of an ice baby, an ice baby that rocks the dreamer and is rocked by the dreamer. The fourth is death by proxy: the vision is of the death of her mother, in which death becomes her mother's child, so that she can be neither her mother's daughter nor her mother's mother. The fifth is death averted: the vision of the attempt to kill death by friendship, a false vision. The sixth is death encountered in vision: death as a baby, to be rocked and to rock, where death is mother to its baby, baby to its mother, in an unending circle of mother and child. The poem is, of course, circular, its end in its beginning, but that is only to be expected in myths.

The poem begins:

I was an ice baby.
I turned to sky blue.
My tears became two glass beads.
My mouth stiffened into a dumb howl.
They say it was a dream
but I remember that hardening.
(1. "Dreams")

Her older sister had dreamed, "nightly," of the death of the new baby: " 'The baby turned to ice. / Somebody put her in the refrigerator / and she turned as hard as a Popsicle.' " But dreams are real experience, says the poem, and so the poet remembers "that hardening." Tears into glass beads, mouth stiffening into howl; and the refrigerator, too, the milk bottle hissing like a snake, caviar turning to lava, because "the rhythm of the refrigerator / had been disturbed" by the alien presence of a dying baby inside. (In yet another of her sister's dreams, the dogs think she is a bone, licking her apart, "loving" her until she is gone.) As always, it is the language of this poetry that effects its transformations. Yet it is difficult now to talk of metaphor or simile. "I was an ice baby"; "I turned to sky blue"; "The tomatoes vomited up their stomachs." Where is the comparison, either explicit or implicit? What is figurative here? Either nothing, or everything; but metaphor's transfer *from* literal *to* figurative is missing. This is, in fact, literal description of a visionary world, where any and all transformations into truth are possible. This is ritual, mantric language, with its significant repetitions and gnomic pronouncements: "I died seven times / in seven ways / letting death give me a sign, / letting death place his mark on my forehead" (3. "Seven Times").

The Dy-dee doll of Part 2 has only two lives. Once the child Anne "snapped / her head off / and let it float in the toilet"; another time she melted under the sun lamp, "trying to get warm."

> She was a gloom,
> her face embracing
> her little bent arms.
> She died in all her rubber wisdom.

The deaths of the doll are another form of experiencing death in imagination and thus without its finality. The doll dies in misery and knowledge, embracing herself.

From the doll's two deaths Sexton moves to her own "seven": the premature or false deaths of attempted suicide. In these attempts, she was getting to know her death, asking for a sign, asking to be marked by death: "And death took root in that sleep," in the dream experience of an ice baby; "and I rocked it / and was rocked by it. / Oh Madonna hold me." The baby is herself; the baby is death.

The most compelling of the poem's six visions are Parts 4 and 6: two pietàs. The fourth, "Madonna," I have called death by proxy; it describes her mother's death, and as any reader of Anne Sexton should know (as most women know), "A woman *is* her mother. / That's the main thing" ("Housewife").[18] Sexton's mother died "unrocked," "thrashing like a fish on the hook": "her rocking horse was pain / with vomit steaming from her mouth." It is a death of horror, for mother and daughter alike. The daughter would help, wants to "place my head in her lap / or even take her in my arms somehow / and fondle her twisted grey hair"; she wants to be mothered, to mother. But death has replaced Anne as her mother's "baby": "Her belly was big with another child, / cancer's baby, big as a football."

What sort of response can be made to death? In Part 5, "Max," the poet and her friend Max make a pact "To beat death down with a stick. / To take over. / To build our death like carpenters." This entails talking turkey, shooting "words straight from the hip" when death comes; not being "polite." The pact, the talks, the conspiracy of the friends, is seen as a means, at first to avert and later to confront death. Yet it is a partial answer only, for in the moment of death one is alone.

The moment of death comes in the vision of Part 6, "Baby." The description of the baby whom the poet rocks concentrates upon its eyes, which are made of glass, "as brittle as crystal." It is the ice baby of the refrigerator dreams, and the baby's sight reveals its knowledge: "Glass eye, ice eye, / primordial eye, / lava eye, / pin eye, / break eye, / how you stare back!" The death baby's gaze is like that of small children, because it knows exactly who she is: it has "worn my underwear," "read my newspaper." Poet and baby rock, locked in a death embrace:

> I rock. I rock.
> We plunge back and forth
> comforting each other.
> We are stone.
> We are carved, a pietà
> that swings and swings . . .
>
> I rock. I rock.
> You are my stone child
> with still eyes like marbles.
> There is a death baby
> for each of us.
> We own him.
> His smell is our smell.
> Beware. Beware.
> There is a tenderness.
> There is a love

for this dumb traveler
waiting in his pink covers.

This is Sexton's winter's tale, a myth that does not praise the new life that must always grow from old life but rather seeks to reconcile the death that also must grow from life. The central actors, and images, of both myths are the same, because both myths are complementary, existing always simultaneously: mother and child, child and mother—this is a woman's myth. One is born with one's death inside oneself, like an egg, or a baby. Through the process of living one transforms oneself into one's own death, through a process of hardening, stiffening, freezing. Each birth only hastens the process, so one grows from baby to child to daughter to mother: in the last act of birth, a mother gives birth to her own death, a death baby. The imagery of the poem underlines the nature of this process, beginning with its initial statement of truth: "I was an ice baby." "Ice," "I," "eyes," are all equated in the poem: death, identity, vision. Even as the ice baby of Part 1 stiffens in that strange morgue, the refrigerator, so the poem's protagonist continues throughout the life of the poem, which follows the temporal course of her life, to stiffen, to grow towards death, until in the final pietà she and the death baby are carved stone, "a pietà / that swings and swings." They are a statue of themselves, their own tombstone. How can stone yet swing and swing? Because *rocking* is the primary act of the poem, an extraordinary pun on the word "rock" that can link stone and maternity. *Rocking*: turning into stone, mothering—I give birth to my own death. I am my mother's baby; I am my mother's death; I am my mother; I am my baby; I am my death. A cold vision, an icy vision, a crystal vision of truth, as Sexton looks into the glass beads of her own eye and finds herself, who is her death, reflected there. These reflections say that the mirroring process cannot go on ad infinitum, for glass turns into stone.

The poem ends this way:

Someday,
heavy with cancer or disaster,
I will look up at Max
and say: It is time.
Hand me the death baby
and there will be
that final rocking.

There is no escaping death, but to know that one can say, "It is time. / Hand me the death baby" indicates that is the only possible way one might yet be powerful. To know and to ask.

Power. The word is everywhere in this essay; the sense of power comes through more and more strongly in the poetry of Anne Sexton. The power comes from making poems that "mean something to someone": from the power of magic, which has always been that of sending words to effect changes, to cause action. The power of the poet whose words are let loose upon the world. Yet the power in Sexton's words comes into them from her insight into herself; from her understanding of her identity in terms of both her own self and the others with whom she interacts, relates. Because she knew who she was, she could give out this knowledge. And the process was wonderfully reciprocal, circular; for she understood who she was with her poems; her words caused her to know who she was. She brought forth from herself the power of her vision, let loose upon the world with words: an egg, a "strange sun"—"the dream, the excitable gift."

Feminine Poetry

Involvement; engagement; commitment—the linking of poetry to experience through the active participation of the poet herself. When the poetry of Levertov, Plath, and Sexton is at its richest and most powerful, it is because such participation occurs. The poet is *in* the poem because she has directly confronted and written out of her own experience of the world. Or, to put it another way, because she has rejected masculine models, techniques, forms, attitudes, when they seem to work at cross-purposes to what she knows and wants to say.

Since the nature of experience itself is to a large extent socially determined, it is not surprising that the forms such poets as Levertov, Plath, and Sexton work in reflect those qualities traditionally associated with women: being personal, particular, concrete, contextual. Both Levertov and Sexton, for example, in their attempts to know themselves (a goal common to both sexes), need to make their definitions in terms of their interpersonal relationships with other people. (Plath arrives at such a stalemate largely because her interpersonal relationships fail her and she has no recourse but solipsism, which to her is a real sign of her defeat as a person. A poet like Wallace Stevens, on the other hand, whose attitudes are similarly solipsistic, is not threatened by that condition. If anything, he feels elevated by it, superior.)

Being concrete, personal, particular, are approaches that occur in a great deal of contemporary poetry; but as I have pointed out earlier, the reasons for and results of such stances may be different for different poets. It is not the same thing to find the universal in the particular as it is to find the particular in the particular. If a woman poet, such as Levertov, wants to link her particular experiences with larger universals—concepts, generalizations—she can call upon only a percentage of her own experiences. Much of what she knows does not link up to universals, because the universals presently in existence are based upon masculine experience, masculine norms. In addition, a poet like Sexton may feel that concepts and generalizations are simply *not necessary* for validity: that her particular communicates by touching the particular in someone else; that generalization obscures and even defeats the poetic event.

The following is a short poem by a young male poet, Gerald Hausman, which in its rendering of experience is both personal and particular.

Sleeping Out

Drunk in a cow meadow
I lay face up, early starshine.
Cows came out of the pine trees
one at a time to stare—
great liquid slow blink eyes,
milkweed breath.
A bold one thrust tongue
to my chin, backed up, puzzled.
Slowly they turned around
tails swishing, and ambled off
tired of flies, false salt blocks
too many milkings.
I stayed and watched, almost drowsing

> until the last white of them
> went out in the dark.[19]

Hausman, like Levertov and many other contemporaries, is writing in the Williams tradition. Where is the generalization? In poems like this one, it is implicit rather than explicit. Partly, it is achieved by his use of figurative language. The cows that the drunken poet sees are linked to all of nature by his language: liquid eyes, milkweed breath, "until the last white of them / went out in the dark"—the pun makes cows into moon and stars. The poet is separate from the cows, from all of nature; he is a "false salt block" who puzzles the cows when they try to lick him, so they back off and leave. He wishes that he were a part of them: when they leave, the white light goes out. Not being one with them, he, as a poet, can observe them in a spirit of sympathy (heightened by his inebriation) and report what he sees, experiences. The entire poem is about the fact that he cannot participate, engage, commit. His experience is that of being unable to engage; of alienation. This particular, personal experience is thus linked to a universal so commonplace as to be cliché: the alienated modern man. The poem also links Gerald Hausman to a long tradition of poets who get drunk and write poems about what they experience in their intoxicated state: again, almost a cliché role for the young poet. How many poems by women are there, I wonder, that begin "Drunk in a cow meadow / I lay face up"?

So I return to the notions about involvement, engagement, commitment—and their converse: distance, objectivity—that have been raised by my discussion of Levertov, Plath, and Sexton. For such women poets this quality of engagement seems essential if their poetry is to fully and truly express their feminine experience. Certainly this is because feminine experience itself is largely defined by the same qualities. Sherry Ortner, in a cross-cultural study of women's roles and their corresponding cognitive modes, defines the (noninnate) female personality as one which "tends to get involved with concrete feelings, things, and people, rather than with abstract entities; it tends towards personalism and particularism."[20] Judith Bardwick's *The Psychology of Women* discusses a quality common in the psychology of women: their lack of an independent sense of self and self-esteem, the fact that they tend to define themselves in terms of their relationships with others—as wife, mother, daughter.[21] A way in which poets like Levertov, Plath, and

Sexton achieve engagement and active participation in their poems is through their use of the persona, that same poetic device that has helped those poets who wanted it to achieve distance and objectivity.

In an essay about the persona and its relation to masculine and feminine literary styles, "Feminist Criticism and the Concept of the Poetic Persona," Marilyn Farwell offers a definition of the persona based upon the writings of some major (male) critics of the twentieth century, including T. S. Eliot, Cleanth Brooks, Robert Penn Warren, and C. S. Lewis.

> The definition of the *persona* entails the separation of various elements of the creative act, of the poet from the speaker of the poem, of the poet who creates from the person who feels, and ultimately of the knower from the known. The original Latin sense of a mask is retained in the New Critical description of the poet who assumes a dramatic mask, who projects another personality in order to control his/her feelings and emotions. . . . It is on the basis of what T. S. Eliot calls the "extinction of personality" that poets of the twentieth century have been evaluated, and this extinction demands the objectification and separation of the personal self from whatever speaker the poem appropriates.[22]

She goes on to describe a very different use of the persona in the work of many women poets:

> The female voice is first of all not objective or analytical, but more likely it will entertain and develop relationship, communication, and identification as poetic devices. The female poet will more often identify the poet and the speaker of the poem, the mind that creates and the woman who suffers, the knower and the known. The separations which we noticed in the definition of the *persona* are the very gaps which the female naturally and the female poet consciously or unconsciously tries to bridge. The "I" of the woman's poetic voice will be visible more often because the defenses which make the male more objective are not part of the female acculturation process. Because the female voice is more aware of psychological events and impressions than of abstract assertions or external dramatic happenings, identity and relationship are the devices of her writing.[23]

A quality that emerges from the best of Levertov, from the later poems of Plath, and from most of the poetry of Sexton is a sense of the writer herself as a person who communicates with and touches other people (readers, listeners) because she involves herself in her poetry. She uses poetry as a means, a way to contact other people. This is a use of that poetic device, the persona. The poem is never "raw" experience itself; it is language that has shaped and ordered experience as it describes it. The voice of the poem must likewise always be both a selection (an aspect of the whole person who is writing) and an artifice, shaped and ordered to suit the needs of the poem. But the selecting and the shaping may create a speaker who is open and intimate; who reveals the self of the writer rather than shields it. The art of Levertov, Plath, and Sexton is often so exciting because this personal quality involves, engages, and commits the reader (as well as the poet) to the poem.

NOTES

1. Barbara Kevles, "The Art of Poetry: Anne Sexton," *Paris Review* 13 (1970–1971): 160–91.
2. Ibid., p. 161.
3. Betty Friedan, *The Feminine Mystique* (New York: W. W. Norton, 1963), p. 11.
4. *To Bedlam and Part Way Back* (Boston: Houghton Mifflin, 1960).
5. *Live or Die* (Boston: Houghton Mifflin, 1966).
6. Kevles, "The Art of Poetry: Anne Sexton," p. 162.
7. *To Bedlam and Part Way Back*, p. 3.
8. *Live or Die*, p. 8.
9. *To Bedlam and Part Way Back*, p. 58.
10. Ibid., p. 17.
11. Ibid., p. 66.
12. Ibid., pp. 51–52.
13. *Love Poems* (Boston: Houghton Mifflin, 1969).
14. *Transformations* (Boston: Houghton Mifflin, 1971).
15. Ibid., p. 44.
16. *The Book of Folly* (Boston: Houghton Mifflin, 1973).
17. *The Death Notebooks* (Boston: Houghton Mifflin, 1974).
18. *All My Pretty Ones* (Boston: Houghton Mifflin, 1961), p. 48.
19. Jean Malley and Halé Tokay, eds., *Contemporaries: Twenty-Eight New American Poets* (New York: The Viking Press, 1972), p. 52.
20. Sherry Ortner, "Is Female to Male as Nature is to Culture?" in Michele Zimbalist Rosaldo and Louise Lamphere, eds., *Women, Culture and Society* (Stanford, California: Stanford University Press, 1974), p. 81.

21. Judith Bardwick, *Psychology of Women* (New York: Harper and Row, 1971), pp. 156, 158.
22. Marilyn Farwell, "Feminist Criticism and the Concept of the Poetic Persona," *Bucknell Review*, in press: 10, 11.
23. Ibid., pp. 16, 17.

7

"A Sweet Inspiration . . . of My People": The Poetry of Gwendolyn Brooks and Nikki Giovanni

In 1972 I heard Gwendolyn Brooks read her poetry at Bucknell University, a small, private, expensive upper-middle-class school in central Pennsylvania. The Black Student Alliance had turned out in full force (some seventy-five people) to pay tribute to this most famous of black poets, the "poet laureate of Chicago." The reading was about blackness, both in the subject matter of the poems and in the ambience of the event itself. The black students were dressed in their finest, not in the jeans they daily wore (the uniform of the white middle-class students to whose school they had been brought), proclaiming that this was their poet and their evening, that tonight we whites were the guests. It was a moving experience, but it was also a full room with poor ventilation, and in spite of myself I grew drowsy. Then Brooks read a poem that woke me abruptly, electrifying me and the rest of the audience with its urgency, its humor, and, above all, its sound. I admit to having thought: now she's really writing what before she was only talking about—and at her age! But it was not her own poem that Brooks had just read. It was her tribute as one black woman poet to another, younger one; a poet who was able to say what she said in the way she said it because Gwendolyn Brooks had lived and written; yet it was a poem that Brooks herself could never have written. It was Nikki Giovanni's "Beautiful Black Men." The differences between these two poets and the links that bind them are the subject of this essay on the black woman poet. Gwendolyn Brooks is the first black woman poet to achieve prominance in twentieth-century America; Nikki Giovanni is one of the most recent. Their sisters include Lucille Clifton, June Jordan, Sonia Sanchez, Mari Evans, Alice Walker, and Johari Amini.

The black woman suffers from not a double but a triple bind. Being doubly oppressed, because of race and sex, she experiences conflict between being poet and woman, poet and black, black and woman. Frequently, she must deal with the issue as one of priorities (which comes first: poet, black, woman?) and of identities (is she a poet who happens to be a black woman, a black who happens to be a woman poet, a woman who happens to be a black poet?). Is it possible to be a black woman poet?

"Queenhood in the new black sun"

Gwendolyn Brooks is the only black woman poet to have achieved public and critical recognition before the 1960's. Her first book of poems, *A Street in Bronzeville*, was published in 1945.[1] It was perhaps only "natural" that the white male literary establishment that published her, reviewed her, and gave her fame (poetry prizes, grants, and the Pulitzer Prize in 1949 for *Annie Allen*)[2] should consider her an "exception," or, more commonly, should consider her neither black nor woman but poet: an American poet who happened to be Negro. Reviews of her work from that early period either ignore the question of race and sex ("These [poems] are mainly about people, the shifting and shabby of a great city, but written out of a background made secure in a careful home by good, intelligent, aware parents")[3] or take special issue with the matter of universality in poetry. For example, J. Saunders Redding, writing on *Annie Allen*, detects the "danger" of her becoming a coterie poet and warns against it:

> The question is . . . whether it is not this penchant for coterie stuff—the special allusions, the highly special feeling derived from an even more special experience—that has brought poetry from the most highly regarded form of communication to the least regarded. No one wants

> to read a psychological treatise, or any treatise whatever for that matter, in order to get at the true meaning of a poem.[4]

He would prefer to emphasize and applaud her style, "as artistically sure, as emotionally fine, as aesthetically complete as a silver figure by Cellini."[5]

It is essential to note that the battle is being waged, and will continue to be waged, over the issue of race, never that of sex. Yet it is especially illuminating to follow the conflict closely, because its attacks and counterattacks, its strategies and slogans, can readily be translated into those that presently engage feminists. It is useful to follow the battle to its conclusion, because of the fact that while the majority of contemporary liberals will now accept its tenets with reference to race, most fail to do so with reference to sex.

As late as 1963, poet Louis Simpson, writing in the New York *Herald Tribune*, dismisses Brooks's achievement because he is "not sure it is possible for a Negro to write well without making us aware he is a Negro; on the other hand, if being Negro is the only subject, the writing is not important."[6] Attack; from the bastions of double discrimination (note the "he" when Simpson is speaking about only Gwendolyn Brooks). Now defense, from a bastion that upon close analysis seems hardly to be the "other side." The speaker is Dan Jaffe, in "Gwendolyn Brooks: An Appreciation from the White Suburb." His position in 1969 is an elaboration of Redding's twenty years earlier. "She has not denied the demands of the Muse for the demands of the Cause":

> She has dealt with black experience honestly and expansively without becoming a sort of poetic pamphleteer. The designation "black poetry" seems to me to be an unfortunate one to attach to her work. The label veils her considerable achievement. I suspect the implications of the term are erroneous.[7]

Jaffe's essay is an extended refutation of the phrase "black poetry" as used, it is important to note, by Brooks herself. Jaffe points to the dubious assumptions behind calling attention to the achievement of "black men," registering the peculiar experiences that set them apart from whites.

> The designation "black poetry" arbitrarily ignores the nature of the creative act and the creative personality and the enormous difficulty of assessing either with certainty. It also ignores what I do not mean to

be a merely facetious observation: the minority of poets is smaller and in some ways (certainly not all) more cohesive than the minority of blacks. It may be that LeRoi Jones and Robert Creeley have more in common than LeRoi Jones and Malcolm X. Nor will any protestation to the contrary by Jones alter this real possibility.

The label "black poetry" suggests that the body of poetry by black poets has certain common characteristics and that these characteristics give the poetry its literary value. If it has no *literary* value we can hardly consider it poetry. Nor can we anticipate that it will have any lasting value. . . .

Certainly ghetto experience has influenced the character of Gwen Brooks' poems. Some will certainly propose that she writes as a black spokesman. But this is a half truth. How she sees and responds reflects her training as a poet as well as the circumstances of her life. When she functions as a poet she changes things. She must see differently not only from whites but from blacks, and especially from other black poets. . . .

What I've said thus far is really a defense of any black poet to be himself first. The label "black poetry" cheapens the achievement of Gwendolyn Brooks. It recommends that race matters more than artistic vocation or individual voice. It would lessen achievements by blacks by supporting a notion of caricature.[8]

Let me permit a powerful and articulate spokesman for the black artist, the poet Don Lee, to defend Brooks and all who use the term "black poetry." Lee's fine essay, "Gwendolyn Brooks: Beyond the Wordmaker—the Making of An African Poet,"[9] traces Brooks's development from a poet who happens to be Negro into a black poet, who can conclude her autobiography with words such as these:

I—who have "gone the gamut" from an almost angry rejection of my dark skin by some of my brain-washed brothers and sisters to a surprised queenhood in the new black sun—am qualified to enter at least the kindergarten of new consciousness now. New consciousness and trudge-toward-progress.[10]

Lee asks, and then answers, the question implicit in the attacks and defenses of Brooks that I have been recording: "How does a black poet (or any black person working creatively) define himself and his work: is he a poet who happens to be black or is he a black man or woman who happens to write?"[11] He counters the "art for art's sake" advocates, both white and black, with another definition of the black artist:

> He is an African in America who expresses himself, his blackness with the written word . . . the creativity that he possesses is a gift that should be shared with his people to the highest level humanly possible. And that this "art" form in some way should be used in the liberation of his people.[12]

Yet Lee is speaking "aesthetically" as well as "politically," because he recognizes the profounder relation between art and politics, that all art is political if only because it gives direction to the future. When he says, "When seeking universality, one always starts with the local and brings to the universal world that which is particularly Russian, Asian, European, Indian, Spanish, African or whatever,"[13] he could be echoing William Carlos Williams ("a local pride"—the first words of *Paterson*). Certainly Williams's Americanism has long been accepted by the literary establishment. Lee's other examples may also be acceptable:

> If one define's oneself as a Russian poet, immediately we know that things that are Russian are important to him and to acknowledge this is not to *leave out the rest of the world* or to limit the poet's range and possibilities in any way . . . .
>
> If a poet defines himself as Chinese we know that the designation carries with it a certain life style which will include Chinese language, dress, cultural mores, feelings, spirituality, music, foods, dance, literature, drama, politics, and so forth. If one is an Indian from India, one is first identified with a *land base*; is identified with a race of people; is identified with all the cultural, religious, and political advantages and disadvantages that are associated with the people whether the "poet" accepts them or not. *This must be understood.*[14]

But the assumption behind his national analogies, that defining oneself from an historical and culturally accurate base and following this through in one's work "gives direction to the coming generations," is not acceptable when it must of necessity question existing structures and demand revolutionary change:

> —people find a sense of *being*, a sense of worth and substance with being associated with *land*. Associations with final roots give us not only a history (which did not start and will not end with this country), but proclaims us heirs to a future and it is best when we, while young, find ourselves talking, acting, living and reflecting in accordance with that future which is best understood in the context of the past.[15]

Race identity—and more recently, sex identity—are threatening in a way that (today, at any rate) national identity is not. When an artist identifies herself or himself with an oppressed group, his creations give reality to that group, and hence to its oppression, as its mere existence does not. Dan Jaffe's own words of argument *against* black poetry explain unwittingly what I am trying to say and point to the basis of his fear:

> If what she presents seems to many of us heightened reality, it is because it is artifice, *the real fashioned and shaped to poetry*. It is both larger and smaller than that outside reality because Gwen Brooks heightens our awareness of its multiplicity, textures, and significances. It is smaller because the totality of the world of flux has too many instances and variables for any human to fully record or comprehend. (my italics)[16]

It was only "natural" that Brooks's early poetry be largely defined by its acceptability. While she never whitewashed her subject matter (her poems have always been about black people, and frequently black women), her style—the manner in which she presented those subjects—was what Lee calls "European," demonstrating her preoccupation with a formal elegance and dexterity directly in the tradition of English literature. Brooks could always be topical or colloquial ("At Joe's Eats / You get your fish or chicken on meat platters"),[17] but such localness was carefully embedded in the universal:

> The pasts of his ancestors lean against
> Him. Crowd him. Fog out his identity.
> Hundreds of hungers mingle with his own,
> Hundreds of voices advise so dexterously
> He quite considers his reactions his,
> Judges he walks most powerfully alone,
> That everything is—simply what it is.
> ("The Sundays of Satin-Legs Smith")

In her early poetry, in other words, Brooks is writing in the English language but not in the language of her own people, which is black English. In Latin and not the vernacular. This is why Lee writes of Pulitzer Prize-winning *Annie Allen*: "Important? Yes. Read by blacks? No. *Annie Allen* more so than *A Street in Bronzeville* seems to have been written for whites. . . . She invents the sonnet-ballad in Part 3 of the poem 'Appendix to the Anniad, leaves from a loose-leaf war diary.' This poem is probably earth-shaking to some, but leaves me completely dry."[18]

Lee's essay is a careful study of Brooks's growth of black consciousness and her corresponding changes in voice and form in keeping with a publicly proclaimed black identity:

> Changes in my work! There *is* something different that I want to do. I want to write poems that will be non-compromising. I don't want to stop a concern with words doing good jobs, which has always been a concern of mine, but I want to write poems that will be meaningful to those people [black people] I described a while ago, things that will touch them.[19]

Her earlier work was "compromising" in the sense that it spoke of blacks to whites, using the white language and poetic tradition to make the black world acceptable. Even as she changed her publisher in 1971 (after twenty-six years with Harper and Row to the black Broadside Press), so she has turned her face into the new black sun and her poetry towards her people. She never has given up English, but her recent poetry has become at the same time more overtly political in theme and both barer and tighter in form.

"Late Annie in her bower lay"

Over the years, Brooks has developed a black consciousness; in her fifties, she opened herself to revolution. But she has not developed at the same time a feminist consciousness. Blackness came and comes first in her life: because race oppression has been the most overt, the most threatening, race identity has also been foremost. She writes: "Black woman must remember, through all the prattle about walking or not walking three or twelve steps behind or ahead of 'her' male, that her personhood precedes her femalehood; that, sweet as sex may be, she cannot endlessly brood on Black Man's blondes, blues, blunders."[20] She has also said: "I think Women's Lib is not for black women for the time being, because black men *need* their women beside them, supporting them in these very tempestuous days. . . . I did say that it's entirely wrong, of course, for women to be denied the same job income men have. When it comes to that, black women should be fighting for equal pay just as white women should."[21] She has a vested interest in women attaining strength and independence, but her interest in them as a group is not political. Women have always been prominent as subject matter for her poems, but she has written about them as about everything else, as subject, never as self.

> Late Annie in her bower lay,
> Though the sun was up and spinning.
> The blush-brown shoulder was so bare,
> Blush-brown lip was winning.
> ("the ballad of late Annie")[22]

> "We use Ardena here." Madame Celeste
> Herself in charge, with hot tough-handed licks
> To tighten contours (Nature wearying)
> Or to release a ropy ruggedness.
> Her stomach sitting softly on her lap,
> Our Mrs. Breck awaits the miracle.
> (*The Anniad*, XII, "beauty shoppe: facial")

> Stand off, daughter of the dusk,
> And do not wince when the bronzy lads
> Hurry to cream-yellow shining.
> It is plausible. The sun is a lode.
>
> True, there is silver under
> The veils of darkness.
> But few care to dig in the night
> For the possible treasure of stars.
> (*The Anniad*, XIII, "intermission, 3")

These examples have been chosen to demonstrate both the range of Brooks's style and also the distance inherent in and essential to her approach. Brooks at no time speaks in a personal or a private voice. She is a dramatic poet, speaking either in the voice of a character (she is especially interested in the dramatic monologue and uses it with skill) or in the voice of an author who does not participate in the drama directly. She regulates tone and point-of-view through her choice of form and phrase, presenting a poem as carefully constructed artifact. She does not speak in the lyric voice, which is, for all that it has been selected and shaped, the voice of the self.

In the passage from "the ballad of late Annie," the regular meter and rhyme, the traditionally poetic phrases for describing heroines—"in her bower lay," "shoulder was so bare"—are employed for the sake of contrast against the "blush-brown" color of the heroine's shoulder and lips. The white language is being used to legitimize a black heroine.

In the "beauty shoppe" passage, both women, Madame Celeste the beautician and Mrs. Breck the customer, are depicted ironically, as is the act in which they are engaged: "Nature wearying," "ropy ruggedness," "miracle." Again, it is the careful phrasing of this strong blank verse that creates tone as well as act.

In the final example, the heightened diction—"daughter of the dusk," "bronzy lads," "veils of darkness," "possible treasure of stars"—is used to validate the black girl as true heroine of this poem. The irony is here directed against the bronzy lads themselves, who cannot see her worth.

When describing an event or person, Brooks will always maintain her authorial distance, so that political or social attitudes are implicit rather than explicit, even in her more recent, more radical pieces. In the following passage from her 1968 volume, *In the Mecca*,[23] Brooks juxtaposes levels of diction to make a statement of value about the action and character being described. Big Bessie is a woman of the people; her name itself, the fact that her feet hurt, the way in which they are hurting ("like nobody's business"), bear witness to this fact. But the nonproletarian vocabulary that is also used to characterize her—"citizen," "highest quality," "admirable," and, especially, the contrast between name and attitude, "Big" and "bigly"—indicates the high stature to be accorded this woman, not in spite of who she is but because of it.

> Big Bessie's feet hurt like nobody's business,
> but she stands—bigly—under the unruly scrutiny, stands in the
> wild weed.
> In the wild weed
> she is a citizen,
> and is a moment of highest quality; admirable.
> ("The Second Sermon on the Warpland, 4")

Often Brooks speaks of women with both compassion and insight. As early as *A Street in Bronzeville*, she writes, in "the mother":

> Abortions will not let you forget.
> You remember the children you got that you did not get,
> The damp small pulps with little or no hair,
> The singers and workers that never handled the air . . .

> I have heard in the voices of the wind the voices of my dim
> killed children.
> I have contracted. I have eased
> My dim dears at the breasts they never could suck.

This dramatic monologue remains one of her most powerful poems, a controversial social statement expressed with eloquence. The theme is that a mother has a blood tie to all of her children, even those that could not be born. The "universality" of the poem's language—"If I poisoned the beginnings of your breaths, / Believe that even in my deliberateness I was not deliberate"—seems meant to ennoble and, again, legitimize, the particular mother in question, who is a black woman talking about abortion—to make reputable the socially disreputable.

Brooks also employs her understanding of her own sex to reveal some of the complex reactions and responses of white women to black women, using the point of view of the white woman herself, as in "A Bronzeville Mother Loiters in Mississippi. Meanwhile, A Mississippi Mother Burns the Bacon," from *The Bean Eaters*[24] or "Bronzeville Woman in a Red Hat" from the same volume.

In the first of these poems, a white woman who has accused a young black man of sexual assault, a "Dark Villain" whom her husband, as "Fine Prince," has murdered, comes to understand the realities of blood and terror that lie beneath her own fantasies of love and marriage, reflecting as they do her culture's equally distorted myths of race and power. In the second, a white mother watches her child, yet innocent of these myths, respond to the love of a black maid:

> Heat at the hairline, heat between the bowels,
> Examining seeming coarse unnatural scene,
> She saw all things except herself serene:
> Child, big black woman, pretty kitchen towels.

Like the white women poets of her generation, Brooks may write about women, but rarely will she include herself among them. She never achieves either the personalism or the engagement that I have identified with the "feminine" poet. Yet there is a difference between her presentation of women and that of the white women poets who are her contemporaries: in Brooks's poetry—and, indeed, throughout the poetry of black women—there is a pride in womanhood that does not exist in the poetry of white women until recently. The white woman poet set herself apart from "women": she was special, because she was a poet. She was not and must not be like those motherly, housewifely, essentially weak creatures whose life-style she repudiated for the sake of her art. The black woman, on the other hand, as wife and mother has been many things but never weak. Her very strength has caused the black male of the sixties and seventies to label her Sapphire: to call her a cause of his own lack of manhood. Indeed! Gwendolyn Brooks, like the black women poets who have followed her, has always expressed pride in the black woman.

> *weaponed woman*
>
> Well, life has been a baffled vehicle
> And baffling. But she fights, and
> Has fought, according to her lights and
> The lenience of her whirling-place.
>
> She fights with semi-folded arms,
> Her strong bag, and the stiff
> Frost of her face (that challenged "When" and "If.")
> And altogether she does Rather Well.[25]

As is customary in Brooks's poetry, the common woman emerges as strong and admirable.

Since the sixties, Brooks has been especially conscious of herself in relation to young blacks. It was they who gave her her new insights into herself and her race; it is they who will win the freedom for which all are fighting. She has talked to them, taught them, joined them, published them, written the best of her new poetry to them. She does not distinguish between their sexes: they are, in the title of the poem from which I quote, "Young Africans."

> *of the furious*
>
> Who take Today and jerk it out of joint
> have made new underpinnings and a Head.
>
> Blacktime is a time for chimeful
> poemhood
> but they decree a
> Jagged chiming now.

And they await,
across the Changes and the spiraling dead,
our black revival, our black vinegar,
our hands, and our hot blood.[26]

"Nikki, / isn't this counterrevolutionary . . . ?"

Nikki Giovanni is one of those "young Africans"; one of those young black poets who come to their craft with that political consciousness regarding the source and purpose of their writing that Don Lee has articulated. She writes:

> Poetry is the culture of a people. We are poets even when we don't write poems; just look at our life, our rhythms, our tenderness, our signifying, our sermons and our songs. I could just as easily say we are all musicians. We are all preachers because we are One. And whatever the term we still are the same in other survival/life tools. The new Black Poets, so called, are in line with this tradition. We rap a tale out, we tell it like we see it; someone jumps up maybe to challenge, to agree. We are still on the corner—no matter where we are—and the corner is in fact the fire, a gathering of the clan after the hunt. I don't think we younger poets are doing anything significantly different from what we as a people have always done. The new Black poetry is in fact just a manifestation of our collective historical needs.[27]

She also comes to her art knowing that she is as female as she is black and that somehow she must, in her own life and art, express how these aspects of herself come together and define her. She has always defined herself as a black woman, seeing Women's Liberation as a white woman's movement; seeing black women as different from both white women and black men: "But white women and Black men are both niggers and both respond as such. He runs to the white man to explain his 'rights' and she runs to us. And I think that's where they are both coming from. . . . We Black women are the single group in the West intact."[28] But her ideas about the black woman's role in the movement have changed over the past several years, I think, moving from a more traditional view (black womanhood comes second to black revolution) to one that is stronger and more individualistic. In *Gemini* she writes: "I don't really think it's bad to be used by someone you love. As Verta Mae pointed out, 'What does it mean to walk five paces behind him?' If he needs to know he's leading, then do it—or stop saying he isn't leading."[29] Yet even at that time, her pride in black women undercuts such a position.

> Because it's clear that no one can outrun us. We Black women have obviously underestimated our strength. I used to think, why don't they just run ahead of us? But obviously we are moving pretty fast. The main thing we have to deal with is, What makes a woman? Once we decide that, everything else will fall into place. As perhaps everything has. Black men have to decide what makes a man.[30]

Two years later, in *A Dialogue*, she argues passionately with James Baldwin: "Black men say, in order for me to be a man, you walk ten paces behind me. Which means nothing. I can walk ten paces behind a dog. It means nothing to me, but if that's what the black man needs, I'll never get far enough behind him for him to be a man. I'll never walk that slowly."[31] Baldwin tries to maintain that black men need black women to give them their manhood *because* the white world takes it away from them. "They've got you; they've got you by the throat and by the balls. And of course it comes out directed to the person closest to you." He says that the woman's role in this civilization is to understand, "to understand the man's point of view," "to understand that although I may love you, in this world I can't come with nothing." He needs to be her *provider*, because only with her can he act like a real man. But Giovanni refuses to allow the man to define her and her role any more. "I've seen so many people get so hung up on such crappy, superficial kinds of things that, for lack of being able to bring a steak in the house, they won't come. I can get my own damn steak." She redefines him: "If the man functions as a man he is not necessarily a provider of all that stuff"; "I'm looking for beauty in the eyes of those I love or want to love, you know? I'm already deprived of almost everything that we find in the world. Must I also be deprived of you?"[32]

> . . . black men—to me, as a woman, which is all I can say—have to say, Okay, I can't go that route; it doesn't work. And it's so illogical to continue to fight that, to continue to try to be little white men. Which is what you're still trying to be. We have our dashikis and your hair is growing, but you're still trying to be little white men. It doesn't work. . . . I demand that you be the man and still not pay the rent. Try it that way.[33]

As a woman, as a black, as a black woman, Giovanni defines herself in terms of two primary factors, which she sees as related: power and love.

> I was trained intellectually and spiritually to respect myself and the people who respected me. I was emotionally trained to love those who love me. If such a thing can be, I was trained to be in power—that is, to learn and act upon necessary emotions which will grant me more control over my life. Sometimes it's a painful thing to make decisions based on our training, but if we are properly trained we do. I consider this a good. My life is not all it will be. There is a real possibility that I can be the first person in my family to be free. That would make me happy. I'm twenty-five years old. A revolutionary poet. I love.[34]

In the relatively brief (I am discussing a five-year period, 1968 to 1972) evolution of her poetry, she develops these attitudes in formal and thematic terms, maturing as a black woman poet.

"Where's your power Black people"

Power and love are what are at issue in Nikki Giovanni's poetry and life. In her earlier poems (1968–1970), these issues are for the most part separate. She writes of personal love in poems of private life; of black power and a public love in political poems. She won her fame with the latter.

> Nigger
> Can you kill
> Can you kill
> Can a nigger kill
> Can a nigger kill a honkie
> Can a nigger kill the Man
> Can you kill nigger
> Huh? nigger can you
> kill
>
> ("The True Import of the Present Dialogue,
> Black vs. Negro")[35]

In poems such as the above, Giovanni speaks for her people in their own language of the social issues that concern them. Her role is that of spokeswoman for others with whom she is kin except for the fact that she possesses the gift of poetry: "i wanted to be / a sweet inspiration in my dreams / of my people . . ." ("The Wonder Woman").[36] The quotation is from a later poem in which she is questioning that very role. But as she gains her fame, the concept of poet as "manifesting our collective historical needs" is very much present.

In defining poetry as "the culture of a people," Giovanni, in the statement from *Gemini* quoted earlier, uses "musician" and "preacher" as synonyms for "poet." All speak for the culture; all *speak*, with the emphasis on the sound they make. Making poems from black English is more than using idioms and grammatical idiosyncrasies; the very form of black English, and certainly its power, is derived from its tradition and preeminent usage as an oral language. So in Giovanni's poems both theme and structure rely on sound patterns for significance.

> i wanta say just gotta say something
> bout those beautiful beautiful beautiful outasight
> black men
> with they afros
> walking down the street
> is the same ol danger
> but a brand new pleasure

In the opening stanza of "Beautiful Black Men (with compliments and apologies to all not mentioned by name),"[37] the idiom ("outasight") is present, so is the special syntax ("they afros"), but more centrally are the rhythms of speech employed to organize the poetic statement. The statement is political, because the poem, like many of hers from this period, is meant to praise blackness: in praising, to foster, to incite. For the proper pride in and achievement of blackness is revolutionary. The poem is not a treatise, however; it is an emotionally charged utterance that, as it develops, creates through its own form the excitement about which it is speaking. In the first stanza, the repetitions, the emphases that the pause at line breaks creates, the accelerations within lines because of lack of pauses, all achieve the tenor of the speaking voice. As the poem progresses, the excitement that the speaker feels as she describes her subject is communicated by her voice on the page:

> sitting on stoops, in bars, going to offices
> running numbers, watching for their whores

preaching in churches, driving their hogs
walking their dogs, winking at me
in their fire red, lime green, burnt orange
royal blue tight tight pants that hug
what i like to hug

The beautiful men are catalogued in action, they then turn and focus on the speaker herself (all of them "winking at me"), and finally they merge into an essence of color, clothing, and sexuality. The verbal process consistently builds image upon image as it accelerates pitch.

jerry butler, wilson pickett, the impressions
temptations, mighty mighty sly
don't have to do anything but walk
on stage
and i scream and stamp and shout

Giovanni becomes quite literally a spokeswoman: she speaks out for black women, appreciating their men now embodied in the musicians who present publicly the image of the black man as a powerful and beautiful star. She raises her voice in praise, screaming, shouting her response.

see new breed men in breed alls
dashiki suits with shirts that match
the lining that complements the ties
that smile at the sandals
where dirty toes peek at me
and i scream and stamp and shout
for more beautiful beautiful beautiful
black men with outasight afros

A sense of humor is never lacking in Giovanni's poetry—serious purpose does not negate the ability to laugh! Here she mocks with affection the black male's love of splendor as it accompanies his dislike of cleanliness. What comes through in her tone is love as well as clear-sightedness, both qualities giving her the right to appreciate "beautiful, beautiful, beautiful black men." From wanting to say, having to say, something about beautiful black men, the poem moves, gathering speed and intensity as it goes, to a scream, a stamp and a shout that impel the person reading to likewise shout, likewise praise—to *feel* as the speaker feels.

Such a feeling is not separate from the one called for in poems like "Poem (No Name No. 2)":

> Bitter Black Bitterness
> Black Bitter Bitterness
> Bitterness Black Brothers
> Bitter Black Get
> Blacker Get Bitter
> Get Black Bitterness
>   NOW
>   (*Black feeling, Black talk/Black judgement*)

—or in "Of Liberation":

> BLACK STEP ONE:
> Get the feeling out (this may be painful—endure)
> BLACK STEP TWO:
> Outline and implement the program
> All honkies and some negros will have to die
> This is unfortunate but necessary
>   (*Black feeling, Black talk/Black judgement*)

For the sound and the feeling go together to create the needed power:

> Honkies always talking 'bout
> Black Folks
> Walking down the streets
> Talking to themselves
> (they say we're high—
> or crazy)
>
> But recent events have shown
> we know who we're talking
> to
>   ("A Short Essay of Affirmation Explaining Why [with Apologies to the Federal Bureau of Investigation]," *Black feeling, Black talk/Black judgement*)

In these early poems, Giovanni is concerned about the political, public implications of her own life, as well; of the fact of her womanhood:

it's a sex object if you're pretty
and no love
or love and no sex if you're fat
get back fat black woman be a mother
grandmother strong thing but not a woman
gameswoman romantic love needer
man seeker dick eater sweat getter
fuck needing love seeking woman
("Woman Poem," *Black feeling, Black talk/Black judgement*)

Using techniques similar to those with which she calls for black power, she can evoke the powerlessness of women. In "All I Gotta Do"[38] phrases that repeat, that halt at line breaks and recur in changing but always inconclusive combinations create Giovanni's frustration at the gap between her individual needs and the means (or lack of them) allotted her by society for fulfilling them. "All i gotta do," "sit and wait," "cause i'm a woman," "it'll find me"—wanting it, needing it, getting it, having it—these are the formulaic phrases. Their arrangement makes the poem.

all i gotta do
is sit and wait
sit and wait
and its gonna find
me
all i gotta do
is sit and wait
if i can learn
how

In stanza 1, the formulaic phrases are used to set out society's rules. The rules do not seem so difficult, the opening phrase attests—"all i gotta do," that's all. Yet a change is rung (through parallel structures) between the hoped-for results (if the game is properly played) that it will "find me" and an inherent difficulty in playing properly: "if i can learn / how." The single word "if," because its setting is so spare, controlled, simple, carries enormous weight: weighing by its problematic stance the *unnatural* societal rules against the natural woman.

what i need to do
is sit and wait
cause i'm a woman
sit and wait
what i gotta do
is sit and wait
cause i'm a woman
it'll find me

In the second stanza, the phrase "sit and wait" occurs three times, a drumbeat behind "need to do," "gotta do," with their causal relation to the central fact supporting the whole enterprise: "cause i'm a woman." Everything follows from that irrevocable fact—especially the end result, "it'll find me": passivity is absolutely necessary for success.

you get yours
and i'll get mine
if i learn
to sit and wait
i want mine
and i'm gonna get it
cause i gotta get it
cause i need to get it
if i learn how

"Sit and wait" continues into the third stanza to remind us of the rules. Another person has been introduced into the poem, someone who does get "his." The urgency of the speaker's own desire for getting is now underlined: "want," "gonna," "gotta," "need to"; and it comes smack up against the terms for carrying desires through: "cause," "cause"—"if."

thought about calling
for it on the phone
asked for a delivery
but they didn't have it
thought about going
to the store to get it
walked to the corner
but they didn't have it

Giovanni's irrepressible humor, the ability to see the comic element present in any life-and-death situation, bubbles to the surface in the fourth stanza, providing, as humor often does, both momentary relief and incisive insight. Calling on the phone, asking for a delivery, walking down to the corner store—acts such as these lead to frustration only. Stores aren't where "it" is found, and, more importantly, one is not supposed to *ask*.

> called your name
> in my sleep
> sitting and waiting
> thought you would awake me
> called your name
> lying in my bed
> but you didn't have it
> offered to go get it
> but you didn't have it
> so i'm sitting

The "you" referred to previously (as having gotten his) now reappears—very obviously a he. "Called your name" becomes a repeated action in the fifth stanza, seemingly a less active kind of initiative-taking than going to the corner store. But it, too, proves unsuccessful, because it is too overt: if asked for it, he doesn't "have it." In such a situation, one should never then offer "to go get it"! "Sitting and waiting," as it repeats and repeats, becomes more and more a plaintive *accusation*.

> all i know
> is sitting and waiting
> waiting and sitting
> cause i'm a woman
> all i know
> is sitting and waiting
> cause i gotta wait
> wait for it to find
> me

The final stanza is formed by the now-familiar formulaic phrases alone—combined, repeated, repeated, combined—and it is this form that creates the poem's concluding sadness, bitterness, and resignation.

"Sitting and waiting" is twice repeated and once reversed, "waiting and sitting." Each phrase is allowed a line to itself, so that the importance of the act is tied to its ceaselessness.

The poem began with the line "all i gotta do." This stanza reorganizes these key words, presenting an opening phrase, "all i know" (the lesson, through the act of the poem, has been thoroughly learned), throwing "gotta" into the seventh line and changing "do" into "wait," thus firmly equating action with nonaction: "cause i gotta wait." The sense of unwavering causation, a train of rules and results whereby society is created (implicit throughout the poem is the double meaning of the word "gotta," linking rule and reward—to have to, to achieve), is finally underlined by the balancing of "cause i'm a woman" with "cause i gotta wait": woman equals waiting. The poem's speaker has learned her lesson: the word "if" no longer appears. What she waits for, "it," has never been defined. It need not be, for the poem has demonstrated that whatever she might want (with whatever degree of intensity) must find her. In the opening stanza, this idea was expressed with an optimism ("its gonna find / me") that was, however, almost immediately undercut by "if i can learn / how." In the last stanza, the uncertainty is expressed with total resignation: "wait for it to find / me." "It" may or may not come, but there is *nothing* the speaker can do about it. Exactly the opposite is required: the less she does do, the more possible becomes the awaited reward; the workings of society are totally out of her hands. The "me" of the poem's last line is alone and alien.

That "me," that lonely woman, is responsible for many private love poems. She seems to have little to do with the spokeswoman who is the black (political) poet. She writes poems like "Rain" from *Re: Creation*.

> rain is
> god's sperm falling
> in the receptive
> woman how else
> to spend
> a rainy day
> other than with you
> seeking sun and stars
> and heavenly bodies
> how else to spend
> a rainy day
> other than with you

These love poems are private and describe the woman enacting rather than criticizing the socially prescribed female role. They speak for Giovanni only and are not meant to incite anybody to any kind of revolution. Such a private/public dichotomy in her work may be neat, but it contains too great a degree of ambivalence for a woman poet like Giovanni to feel comfortable with it or to maintain it for long. How can the woman who sees herself as a sweet inspiration of her people and the woman who has been trained not only to sit and wait but also to need and to value interpersonal, private relationships be the same poet? In "Adulthood" (*Black feeling, Black talk/Black judgement*), she writes about going to college and learning that "just because everything i was was unreal / i could be real"—not from "withdrawal / into emotional crosshairs or colored bourgeois / intellectual pretensions," "But from involvement with things approaching reality / i could possibly have a life." What about not merely black reality, but her own reality? And what is the relation between them? Especially as through her poetry she becomes a genuine public personality, she needs to ask these questions. And what about the revolution?

"dreams of being a natural / woman"

A poet may be musician, preacher, articulator of a culture, but she or he is also a dreamer. In a series of poems about herself as dreamer, Giovanni explores the conflicting and confusing relations between her roles as poet, woman, and black.

In "Dreams" (*Black feeling, Black talk/Black judgement*), she describes her younger years—"before i learned / black people aren't / supposed to dream." She wanted, she says, to be a musician, a singer, a Raelet or maybe Marjorie Hendricks, grinding up against the mike screaming "baaaaaby nightandday." But then she "became more sensible":

> and decided i would
> settle down
> and just become
> a sweet inspiration

(The significance of the black singer—the musician as articulating the culture—appears throughout her work, as in "Revolutionary Music":

"you've just got to dig sly / and the family stone / damn the words / you gonna be dancing to the music" . . . "we be digging all / our revolutionary music consciously or un / cause sam cooke said 'a change is gonna come.' ")[39]

A few years later, in "The Wonder Woman" (*My House*), she must deal with the fact of having become that sweet inspiration. "Dreams have a way / of tossing and turning themselves / around," she observes; also that "the times / make requirements that we dream / real dreams." She may have once dreamed of becoming a sweet inspiration of her people:

> . . . but the times
> require that i give
> myself willingly and become
> a wonder woman.

The wonder woman is a totally public personage who cannot—must not—integrate her personal needs and experiences into that role if they do not coincide. Giovanni makes this clear in poems about female stars, like Aretha Franklin, and in poems about herself, such as "Categories" (*My House*).

> sometimes you hear a question like "what is
> your responsibility as an unwed mother"
> and some other times you stand sweating profusely before
> going on stage and somebody says "but you are used
>   to it"
> or maybe you look into a face you've never seen
> or never noticed and you know
> the ugly awful loneliness of being
> locked into a mind and body that belong
> to a *name* or *non-name*—not that it matters
> cause *you* feel and *it* felt but you have
> a planetrainbussubway—it doesn't matter—something
> to catch to take your arms away from someone
> you might have thought about
> putting them around if you didn't
> have all that shit to take you safely away

"Categories" goes on to question even black/white divisions (political and public), if they can—and they do—at times violate personal reality, describing in its second stanza an old white woman "who maybe you'd really care about" except that, being a young black woman, one's "job" is to "kill maim or seriously / make her question / the validity of her existence."

The poem ends by questioning the fact and function of categories themselves (". . . if this seems / like somewhat of a tentative poem it's probably / because i just realized that / i'm bored with categories"), but, in doing so, it is raising the more profound matter of the relations between society and self. The earlier "Poem for Aretha," 1970 (*Re: Creation*), begins with a clear sense of the separation between public and private selves:

> cause nobody deals with Aretha—a mother with four
>   children—having to hit the road
> they always say "after she comes
> home" . . .

Again Giovanni explains the significance of the musician/artist to society: "she is undoubtedly the one person who puts everyone on / notice," but about Aretha she also says, "she's more important than her music—if they must be / separated." (It is significant that the form of both these poems is closer to thought than speech. No answers here, only questions, problems.)

One means of bridging the gap between public and private is suggested in "Revolutionary Dreams," 1970 (*Re: Creation*).

> i used to dream militant
> dreams of taking
> over america to show
> these white folks how it should be
> done
> i used to dream radical dreams
> of blowing everyone away with my perceptive powers
> of correct analysis
> i even used to think i'd be the one
> to stop the riot and negotiate the peace
> then i awoke and dug
> that if i dreamed natural
> dreams of being a natural
> woman doing what a woman

does when she's natural
i would have a revolution

"Militant" and "radical" are poised against "natural" here, as they were in "Categories." But this poem makes the connection to gender: the "natural dreams," of a "natural woman" who does what a woman does "when she's natural." The result of this juxtaposition is "true revolution." Somehow the black woman must be true to herself as she *is* to be both a poet and a revolutionary, for the nature of the revolution itself is in question. Revolutions are not only in the streets, where niggers must be asked if they can kill. Revolutions do not occur only in male terms, as Giovanni had begun to understand, humorously, in "Seduction" (*Black feeling, Black talk/Black judgement*), in which the male keeps talking politics ("The Black . . ."; "The way I see we ought to . . ."; "And what about the situation . . ."; "the revolution . . .") while she is resting his hand on her stomach, licking his arm, unbuckling his pants, taking his shorts off. The poem is, however, set in some hypothetical future: "one day." It concludes with that future:

then you'll notice
your state of undress
and knowing you you'll just say
"Nikki,
isn't this counterrevolutionary . . .?"

The implicit reply is no, but it is not until her 1972 volume, *My House*, that Giovanni can make this answer with self-confidence. In the poems of *Black feeling, Black talk/Black judgement* and of *Re: Creation*, the doubts are present, and possibilities for solution occur and disappear. However, *My House* as a book, not only the individual poems in it, makes a new statement about the revolution, about the very nature of political poetry, when the poet is a black woman.

Earlier, in "My Poem" (*Black feeling, Black talk/Black judgement*), she had written:

the revolution
is in the streets
and if i stay on
the 5th floor
it will go on
and if i never do

anything
it will go on

Perhaps, but it will not be the same revolution, she has realized; and she has also come to understand that it will take place, as well, on the fifth floor.

In "On the Issue of Roles," Toni Cade, editor of one of the first collections of essays about being black and female, *The Black Woman*, makes a comment that seems to me to be a valuable gloss to the statement of Giovanni's *My House*.

> If your house ain't in order, you ain't in order. It is so much easier to be out there than right here. The revolution ain't out there. Yet. But it is here. Should be. And arguing that instant-coffee-ten-minutes-to-midnight alibi to justify hasty-headed dealings with your mate is shit. Ain't no such animal as an instant gorilla.[40]

Ida Lewis points with a different vocabulary to the same phenomenon: "A most interesting aspect of her [Giovanni's] work is the poet's belief in individualism at a time when the trend in the Black community is away from the individual and towards the mass."[41] In *My House*, Giovanni is trying to be a natural woman doing what a woman does when she's natural—in doing so, dreaming natural dreams, having a revolution. She is integrating private and public; in doing so, politicizing the private, personalizing the public. This action is occurring in poetry.

My House is divided into two sections, "The Rooms Inside" and "The Rooms Outside." The inside rooms hold personal poems about grandmothers, mothers, friends, lovers—all in their own way love poems. "Legacies," in which the poet describes the relationship between grandmother and granddaughter, is a very political poem.

> "i want chu to learn how to make rolls" said the old
> woman proudly
> but the little girl didn't want
> to learn how because she knew
> even if she couldn't say it that
> that would mean when the old one died she would be less
> dependent on her spirit so
> she said
> "i don't want to know how to make no rolls"

Black heritage is explained in personal terms. The little girl in the poem recognizes an impulse to be independent, but the speaker recognizes as well the importance of the old woman, of her love, to the grandchild in achieving her own adulthood. Although the poem ends by observing that "neither of them ever / said what they meant / and i guess nobody ever does," it is the poem itself that provides that meaning through its understanding.

Overtly political are poems like "Categories" or "The Wonder Woman," but also political are the gentle love poems ("The Butterfly," "When I Nap"), and indeed all the poems that are about Giovanni as private person; for in various dialogues and dialects they all make this statement:

> . . . i'm glad
> i'm Black not only
> because it's beautiful but because it's me
> and i can be dumb and old and petty and ugly
> and jealous but i still need love
> ("Straight Talk")

The poems of the rooms outside are not calls to action from the public platform; they are dreams, some funny, some apocalyptic, of old worlds and new. In each of these poems, *My House*'s equivalent to the earlier poems of black feeling and black judgment, the poet stresses the element of personal vision.

> the outline of a face on a picture isn't really
> a face or an image of a face but the idea of an image
> of a dream that once was dreamed by some artist
> who never knew how much more real is a dream than reality
>
> so julian bond was elected president and rap brown chief
> justice of the supreme court and nixon sold himself
> on 42nd street for a package of winstons
> (with the down home taste) and our man on the moon said
> alleluia
> and we all raised our right fist in the power sign
> and the earth was thrown off course and crashed into the sun
> but since we never recognize the sun
> we went right on to work in our factories
> and offices and laundry mats and record shops

the next morning and only the children
and a few poets knew
that a change had come

("Nothing Makes Sense")

This artist has begun to learn—through a process of coming to terms with herself as black woman, black poet, that art can create as well as reflect reality, as revolutions do.

It is fitting to the purpose of *My House* that its final poem, which is in "The Rooms Outside," is "My House."

i only want to
be there to kiss you
as you want to be kissed
when you need to be kissed
where i want to kiss you
cause it's my house
and i plan to live in it

The first stanza follows Giovanni's familiar oral structure. Phrases stand against one another without the imaginative extensions of figurative language: word against word, repeating, altering, pointing. A love poem, to one particular lover. It starts in a tone reminiscent of both "Beautiful Black Men" and "all i gotta do"—the woman is there to adore her man: "i only want to / be there to kiss you"; "as you want"; "as you need." But although the gentle tone persists, an extraordinary change is rung with a firm emphasis on the personal and the possessive in the last three lines: "where i want to kiss you," "my house," "i plan." She is suiting his needs to hers as well as vice versa.

i really need to hug you
when i want to hug you
as you like to hug me
does this sound like a silly poem

In terms of one (important) action, hugging—touching—the point is clarified. The woman of "all i gotta do" has forgotten, or chosen to forget, the rules!

i mean it's my house
and i want to fry pork chops
and bake sweet potatoes

and call them yams
cause i run the kitchen
and i can stand the heat

Nonetheless, she makes it clear that she is still very much of a woman, using the traditionally female vocabulary of cooking and kitchens to underscore her message. But this woman is active, not passive: she means, wants, bakes, calls, runs. She orders experience and controls it. The element of control asserts itself not only through direct statement—"cause i run the kitchen"—but through vocabulary itself: "i mean"; "[i] call them yams" (in the latter phrase asserting blackness itself through control of language: "yams" and not "sweet potatoes"). She controls not only through need and desire but through strength, ability: "i can stand the heat."

i spent all winter in
carpet stores gathering
patches so i could make
a quilt
does this really sound
like a silly poem
i mean i want to keep you
warm

For love is not unrelated to action, strength, control. All of these qualities can be directed to that end in a significant way: "i want to keep you / warm." Gathering patches; no longer waiting for "it" to find her. And making poems about gathering patches—is that silly?

and my windows might be dirty
but it's my house
and if i can't see out sometimes
they can't see in either

The house and its elements are beginning to assume symbolic proportions, surely emphasized by the fact that the poem has been continually calling attention to its existence as a poem. The house is a world; it is reality.

english isn't a good language
to express emotion through
mostly i imagine because people

try to speak english instead
of trying to speak through it
i don't know maybe it is
a silly poem

I am making a message, both poet and poem are insisting; and now they explain how messages work. "Trying to speak through" language rather than speaking it means that word and thing are not identical: that words are not yams, and thus language frees the poet to create realities (dreams) and not just to copy them. So that somehow this not-very-silly poem is carrying out a revolution.

i'm saying it's my house
and i'll make fudge and call
it love and touch my lips
to the chocolate warmth
and smile at old men and call
it revolution cause what's real
is really real
and i still like men in tight
pants cause everybody has some
thing. to give and more
important need something to take

and this is my house and you make me
happy
so this is your poem

The act of naming, of using language creatively, becomes the most powerful action of all—saying, calling. Calling fudge love, calling smiling at old men revolution is creative (rather than derivative) action that expresses more than her own powers as woman and poet. In "Seduction" there was a significant gap between language (rhetoric) and action, between male and female. In that fable, men and words were allied and were seen by the woman poet as impotent. The woman was allied with action (love), but she was, in the poem, mute. The man calls her action "counterrevolutionary." Now, in "My House," the woman's action, love (an overt expression of the personal, private sphere), is allied to language. Giovanni brings her power bases together in this poem, her dominion over kitchens, love, and words. No longer passive in any way, she makes the food, the love, the poem, and the revolution. She brings together things and words through her own vision (dream, poem) of them, seeing that language (naming) is action, because it makes things happen. Once fudge has been named love, touching one's lips to it becomes an act of love; smiling at old men becomes revolution "cause what's real / is really real." Real = dream + experience. To make all this happen, most of all there must exist a sense of self on the part of the maker, which is why the overriding tone of the poem is the sense of an "i" who in giving need feel no impotence from the act of taking (both become aspects of the same event). Thus this is *her* house and he makes her happy, thus and only thus—"cause" abounds in this poem, too: this, her poem, can be his poem. Not silly at all.

In bringing together her private and public roles and thereby validating her sense of self as black woman poet, Giovanni is on her way towards achieving in art that for which she was trained: emotionally, to love; intellectually and spiritually, to be in power; "to learn and act upon necessary emotions which will grant me more control over my life," as she writes in *Gemini*. Through interrelating love and power, to achieve a revolution—to be free. She concludes her poem "When I Die" (*My House*) with these lines:

> and if i ever touched a life i hope that life knows
> that i know that touching was and still is and will always
>   be the true
> revolution

These words of poetry explain the way to enact a dream, one that is "a real possibility": "that I can be the first person in my family to be free . . . I'm twenty-five years old. A revolutionary poet. I love."[42]

Wherever Nikki Giovanni's life as poet will take her, she will go there in full possession of her self. Rather than reiterating the fact of Gwendolyn Brooks in that admirable achievement, let me conclude with Giovanni's poem "For Gwendolyn Brooks."

> brooks start with cloud condensation
> allah crying
> for his lost children
>
> brooks babble
> from mountain tops to settle
> in collecting the earth's essence

pure spring fountain
of love knowledge
for those who find
and dare drink
of it

(*Re: Creation*)

NOTES

1. *A Street in Bronzeville* (New York: Harper and Row, 1945).
2. *Annie Allen* (New York: Harper and Row, 1949).
3. Eloise Perry Hazard, "A Habit of Firsts," *Saturday Review of Literature* 33, no. 2 (May 20, 1950): 23.
4. J. Saunders Redding, *Saturday Review of Literature* 32, no. 38 (September 17, 1949): 23.
5. Ibid., p. 23.
6. Quoted by Stephen Henderson in *Understanding the New Black Poetry* (New York: William Morrow, 1973), p. 7.
7. Dan Jaffe, "Gwendolyn Brooks: An Appreciation from the White Suburb," in C. W. E. Bigsby, ed., *The Black American Writer* (Deland, Florida: Everett Edwards, 1969), p. 90.
8. Ibid., pp. 90–92.
9. Don Lee, "Gwendolyn Brooks: Beyond the Wordmaker—the Making of an African Poet," prefacing Gwendolyn Brooks, *Report from Part One* (Detroit: Broadside Press, 1972), pp. 13–30.
10. Brooks, *Report from Part One*, p. 86.
11. Lee, "Gwendolyn Brooks: Beyond the Wordmaker—the Making of an African Poet," Brooks, *Report from Part One*, p. 26.
12. Ibid., p. 26.
13. Ibid., p. 27.
14. Ibid., pp. 26, 27.
15. Ibid., p. 28.
16. "Gwendolyn Brooks: An Appreciation from the White Suburb," Bigsby, ed., *The Black American Writer*, p. 92.
17. "The Sundays of Satin-Legs Smith," *Selected Poems* (New York: Harper and Row, 1963), p. 17.
18. Lee, "Gwendolyn Brooks: Beyond the Wordmaker—the Making of an African Poet," Brooks, *Report from Part One*, p. 17.
19. Brooks, *Report from Part One*, p. 152.
20. Ibid., p. 204.

21. Ibid., pp. 179–80.
22. *Annie Allen*, p. 10.
23. *In the Mecca* (New York: Harper and Row, 1968).
24. *The Bean Eaters* (New York: Harper and Row, 1960).
25. *Selected Poems*, p. 125.
26. *Family Pictures* (Detroit: Broadside Press, 1970), p. 18.
27. *Gemini: An Extended Autobiographical Statement on My First Twenty-Five Years of Being a Black Poet* (New York: The Viking Press, 1971), pp. 95–96.
28. Ibid., p. 144.
29. Ibid., p. 144.
30. Ibid., p. 145.
31. *A Dialogue* (New York and Philadelphia: J. B. Lippincott, 1973), p. 31.
32. Ibid., pp. 46–55.
33. Ibid., p. 66.
34. *Gemini*, p. 33.
35. *Black feeling, Black talk/Black judgement* (New York: William Morrow, 1970), p. 19.
36. *My House* (New York: William Morrow, 1972), p. 28.
37. *Black feeling, Black talk/Black judgement*, p. 77.
38. *Re: Creation* (Detroit: Broadside Press, 1971), pp. 25–26.
39. *Black feeling, Black talk/Black judgement*, p. 75.
40. Toni Cade, "On the Issue of Roles," in Toni Cade, ed., *The Black Woman* (New York: New American Library, 1970), p. 110.
41. Ida Lewis, Introduction to *My House*, p. xiii.
42. *Gemini*, p. 33.

8

The Feminist Poet: Alta and Adrienne Rich

The feminist poet finds "woman" and "poet" to be political words. Through art that reflects, expresses, creates her life, she both validates herself as she is and works towards the revolution, the transformations that she desires: "breaking down the artificial barriers between private and public, between Vietnam and the lovers' bed" (Adrienne Rich).[1]

Writing poems from personal experience, feminine experience is an act both necessary and vital to the revolution that is occurring. This revolution must begin in the mind, for consciousness needs to be raised before public change can take place. Consciousness of oppression; consciousness of identity. As long as women believe in the definition of themselves created by a male culture, they can not know themselves to be oppressed. People born to be slaves, who need and want other people to "take care of" them, who see themselves as inferior, are by definition not oppressed when others allow them to play out this role. Step 1 has been to realize that women are not what we have been told about ourselves. Step 2 is to find out who we are. Starting all over again. We need before us the evidence in many forms of women and their lives. Feminist poets are giving us these lives.

The life that she will offer needs not only to be validated; it needs to be changed. As feminists, we work for affirmative action and child care centers, but we work as well at individual lives. The poems that feminists write are acts that change their lives; change, also, the lives of those who read and hear. Through seeing who we are, we change; through saying who we are, we change; through seeing and saying who we might become, we start to change into her.

Yet although women share much because of the fact of their sex, each woman encounters feminine experience with her own individuality. Consequently, the forms that women seek in art for expressing that experience must of necessity be varied. Finding oneself means finding one's own voice; and this voice, to turn into a poem, must, in Adrienne Rich's words, be that "of someone who knows the rhythm of his or her own energy and blood."[2] There is no one rule for feminine form, precisely because it needs to be an articulation of the person, an extension of the person. Yet this very commitment to the self in poetry is feminine and feminist. The need to validate the personal and the private as legitimate topics for public speech is particularly feminine; the need to integrate the private and the public is particularly feminist: "But I don't see a radical feminism as preceding from anything but a connection between inner and outer. We are attempting, in fact, to break down that fragmentation of inner and outer in every possible realm. The psyche and the world out there are being acted on and interacting intensely all the time" (Adrienne Rich).[3] The rules for the private sphere (woman's place) have heretofore not applied to the public sphere (man's world). Now feminist poets are working to integrate their own lives and that of the world.

In the late sixties and early seventies, an explosion of poetry by women occurred: existing writers have been discovered, new writers have been published. Certainly, this interest in women poets has been related to the existence of the women's movement at large. Certainly, women writers are being published today who would not have been ten years ago. Yet this fact does not itself prove faddishness or lack of quality in such work. It points rather to changes in the very way in which poetry is being evaluated. The recognition that women *can* be poets acknowledges as legitimate poetry with themes hitherto omitted from the canon, or familiar themes treated from a different perspective. It acknowledges as well changes in poetic form: "but is it poetry?"

Recently, I received a rejection slip from a well-meaning editor who, while admitting the "necessary" nature of my poems, took issue with the fact that my poems "said it all." "Try more denotation . . . synecdoche, metonymy, suggestion," he said. Yet I and many feminist poets do not want to treat poetry as a metalanguage that needs to be decoded to reveal meaning. Poetic language must always be language, not the "thing," so that what we call poetry is made from the inevitable yet always wonderful tension that exists between body acts and language acts. Among many feminist poets, however, there is a need to reveal rather than to conceal, to use a language bare not only of adornment but of obliqueness.

Mary Mackey, in "Women's Poetry: Almost Subversive," describes recent poetry by women this way:

> . . . right off the bat they tend to commit the unpardonable sin of speaking clearly. Poems by women often make statements that can be understood by everyone, statements like:
>
> I have no color belt in karate.
> I only know how to kill.
>
> Why a poem as blunt as that is positively unprofessional. A six year old could read it. If everyone went around writing poetry like that, they'd have to give up teaching it in the universities. Obviously the woman who produced it must be a bit simple-minded. Apparently she had blithely assumed the relation between poet and reader must be one of equality rather than between priest and worshipper.
>
> Speak clearly? Right out of your own life? It's naked, indecent, obviously unpublishable. Besides, sometimes a poem that doesn't hide behind symbols, tropes, and obscure allusions sounds a little clumsy, a little plain.
>
> Clumsy like a scream.[4]

Mackey is pointing to another way in which feminist poetry is a political act. In speaking as it does, it alters the communication between poet and reader/listener itself in accordance with feminist values, promoting nonhierarchical interchange rather than a power trip. Mackey observes that poetry by men has always been part and agent of the patriarchy:

> Because to be published a poem must be obscure, symbolic, magical, abstract, inaccessible. If it contains a few words in Sanskrit or an indirect reference to a 16th century Moldavian archivist, so much the better. A poem, to be published, must make the reader feel overawed, inadequate, a little thick-headed; it must, in turn, make the poet seem superior, in control, a high priest whose talent, art, and knowledge are beyond those of the ordinary person.[5]

Now, however, women poets are beginning to be published, and one reason is that there is a visibly expanding audience for their work: so many women who always thought that "poetry had nothing to say to me" are hungrily reading and asking for more names. More importantly, perhaps, women are publishing themselves. Women's presses and periodicals now exist throughout the country so that women's voices can be heard. Some of the most radical of these voices are not yet listened to at the New York publishing houses (and some, like Judy Grahn or Susan Griffin, do not want to be published by the very establishment against which they are in revolt), but the readers care little about where the book comes from; they are concerned with what it says.

Women's voices in poetry are high and low, elegant and harsh. Sometimes they talk, sometimes they sing, but they tend to share two characteristics: they are strong and real. Alta and Adrienne Rich can represent two extremes of feminist poetry: the distilled colloquial of Alta, whose emotions are on the surface of her skin and her poems; the surrealism of Rich, whose words are pared and chiseled to the cold bone of vision. I chose them from among many: Erica Jong, Diane Wakoski, Susan Griffin, Judy Grahn, Kathleen Fraser, Marge Piercy, Robin Morgan, Margaret Atwood, Lynn Strongin, Lynn Sukenick, Lynn Lifshin, and others whose work continues to surface.

Alta: "i stand in my own pain / & sing my own song"

Alta was a feminist poet way back when (in the sixties!) there was not so much company. In 1969 she founded and still operates one of the country's first feminist presses, Shameless Hussy Press.

Euridice

all the male poets write of orpheus
as if they look back & expect
to find me walking patiently
behind them. they claim i fell into hell.
damn them, i say.
i stand in my own pain
& sing my own song.[6]

It is only recently that she has been represented in any national anthologies, a recognition that has come from women.[7] An important fact, because the most common negative response to her poetry is: "It isn't poetry." Who says? People who don't like what she writes—a vicious kind of circle. Don't *like* it (we are now at an emotional, not an intellectual or theoretical, level) because it is shocking. Why shocking? In its anger (and joy) it does not lie. It isn't true life, it is poetry, but the electric connection between the two kinds of truth is not severed. For some, the poems are too honest: "how can i do this? / how can i write this need? / have i no shame?" she herself asks.[8] But it is necessary that the need be written: "because my song is my life / & you cant have just my poems. / we're a package deal." (The title of the poem quoted makes a telling comment: "—we want yr words, alta, we just dont want you.—woman on the staff of it aint me, babe.")

Honest, these poems lack "decorum," that heretofore primary criterion for women's language. They shock when they speak to men (in this case, her husband): "take me to the woods sometime instead of / your girlfriend / see how you like it." They shock more profoundly when they speak to women—not through men, because of men, about men, or for men—but to women directly.

> can we speak true & trust?
> what is this need i have
> to know a woman as friend?
> to know you, andrea, as well as
> i know the pain in yr poems.
>
> where are you turning we're
> opening we're opening hold
> my hand my body's opening[9]

They shock not only because they overturn stereotypical male/female relationships, but because they break down all protective barriers of politeness that isolate one human from another:

> i havent written about this
> because its going to hurt.
> it's going to hurt her & it's
> going to hurt me.
> she's never said

> "stop being racist"
> & i've never said
> "do i act like i been raised
> english?"
> i call her when i'm in trouble,
> but it was 2 years
> before i went to see her in her home.
> ("Alchemy," I, *I am Not a Practicing Angel*)

A Confusion of Musk

> when we knelt side by side
> the smell of us rose between our legs
> & i couldnt tell, after the first shock
> (that means i want her!)
> i couldnt tell if it were yrs or mine.
> (*I Am Not a Practicing Angel*)

Alta writes of the moments we try to ignore or forget about ourselves and others ("ever since i suggested / we make love / she hasnt let me / touch her / am i so vile"), because she is fighting a revolution that is not only for women but for love itself: "so that we are both fully exposed, & vulnerable to each others love."[10]

Alta is shocking for another reason: she is funny.

> euch, are you having yr *per*iod?
> why didn't you *tell* me?
> i shoulda fucked him ina dark.
> he coulda thot bloody sheets
> look ma a virgin
> (*No Visible Means of Support*)

> if yr not good to me,
> you'll have to watch your step.
> i have friends in low places.
> (*I Am Not a Practicing Angel*)

> i beat off after every meal.
> havent had a cavity for years!
> (*I Am Not a Practicing Angel*)

There is always a gasp of pain in our laughter for these poems, as there is in Alta's wry wit when she writes them. It is allowable for people in pain to laugh at themselves (it eases the hurt and keeps them from resisting), but they are not supposed to use their humor as a way of fighting back. Alta's wit threatens, because it helps bring pain into full consciousness, which is the first step.

Elaine Gill calls Alta's lyrics "terse" and "pure."[11] It is the distillation of experience that her words achieve that accounts for this purity; it is their engagement with experience at a level of direct feeling that accounts for the terseness.

> first pregnancy:
> lonely & big
> a couple of time i cried
> hearing you
> beating off under covers.
> (*Song of the Wife/Song of the Mistress*)

> you think weeping sounds bad,
> you should hear me laugh
> (*No Visible Means of Support*)

> *To My Children on a Trip*
>
> they don't need my fear
> riding along with them
> like an unwanted ghost.
> (*No Visible Means of Support*)

The compression in such poems results in an accompanying expansion, which however takes place in the mind of the reader/listener. I am talking about the impact from these poems, an afterimage or aftertaste, a reverberation that occurs when the poem *connects* to a place of feeling within me.

But is it poetry?

> this ain't a poem, it's just something i have to say:
> if yr planning an abortion, because yr afraid
> of social censure, or afraid you wont be able
> to support yr child, don't do it.
> society is what has to give,
> not our children.
> (*I Am Not a Practicing Angel*)

In a prose article on women's poetry, "TELL IT LIKE IT IS," she also discusses this question:

> IT'S DIFFICULT TO BE CLEAR & NOT ONE DIMENSIONAL. ONLY A GREAT WRITER CAN DO IT. SO MANY POEMS ARE JUST STATEMENTS: WITH POLITICS BEHIND THEM, IT DOESNT REALLY MATTER IF THEYRE TIMELESS ART. BUT THESE POEMS ARE VALID NOW, & THEY SHOULD BE HEARD NOW. THE POEMS PEOPLE NEED IN 2072, THEY'LL READ (I HOPE) IN 2072. & I HOPE A LOT OF THE BATTLES WE'RE FIGHTING NOW WILL BE WON, EVEN IF IT MEANS 1/2 OUR WORK WILL BE IRRELEVANT. WE MUST WORK TOWARDS OUR OWN OBSOLESCENCE.[12]

With a strong political imperative behind her work, Alta is making a distinction, not between poems and nonpoems, but between time-bound and timeless art. She is writing, not for eternity, but for now. Yet when Alta is very good, and often she is, her poems express the human spirit on a level that might very well be timeless—who can know? What her comment and the poem quoted above underline is the reason why, for any superior poem on a page, there are others less successful, because they don't work (at the level of distilling and integrating language and experience) so well. They are there on the page anyway, because they continue to be "something i have to say." For Alta, that is sufficient reason for their presence.

Alta's poems come out of private and politicized woman's experience. She writes to and about her lovers (female and male), children, friends, and enemies; she writes out of longing, anger, pain, desire, frustration, joy, loneliness, bitterness, pride. These intensely personal emotions are political, because Alta is conscious of the fact that her own suffering can speak to others, too; that ultimately it must speak to others if ever it is to be overcome.

> the wound of crying alone.
> of being the voice that fits no ear.
> no shelled ear catching the screech
> of this wound, the wound of hearing our own
> screams uninterrupted,
> bouncing back from concrete & glass
> & our ears ache & our throats crack dry &
> only the other screams that sometimes bounce

back from other concrete walls interrupt
our pain / & the double pain easier because
another spirit wants out, another
person in pain wants to care &
the wounded recognize each other.
our wounds will heal us.
("The Wound Will Heal Us")[13]

Poetry is a way of speaking: "your tiny body warms my breast"; "i promised i would but i can't. So what else is new?"; "if you won't make love to me, at least / get out of my dreams!" It is the poem itself that serves as the agent of connection between people. For the poem to work, the reader/listener has to take part (as herself/himself, as the person to whom the poem is addressed, as the speaker of the poem). To cause such response, this kind of poem usually does not use the imaginative transformations of figurative language. Rather, it calls on the impact of the literal detail to fly directly like an arrow, to touch feeling to feeling. There is in such poetry an inherent distrust of a language (a sexist language) that has always before been used to deceive, to distance, to separate: "my history books lied to me. they said i didn't exist"; "-dont tell anyone about our affair. i intend to run for city council.- / -bob."

how can i reach out with poetry
when words are such faulty fingers?

To work, poetry must be removed from the realm of "fantasy": "come honest to the bone. / peel away the lies / (i'm afraid)," she writes in a poem called "ITS THE REAL THING IN THE BACK OF YOUR MIND." A difficult thing to do: "its not that i lie, its just / sometimes i like to hide a little bit. / that's a lie, i dont like / to have to hide at all." But this poem itself persists in revealing, baring its speaker as it, and she, look at her hands, with nails that aren't pretty, hands that "are strong & can make music / & fix a press"; at her titties that are "funny" because "those children loved my milk"; at her scarred skin and high cheekbones:

. . . i dont
look like what youve been taught to want.
my body looks like me, like a strong woman
who has survived a lot & come out

dancing.
here i am.
(i'm afraid)
here i am . . .

it's my face & i stand behind it.
here i am.

It is the poem that brings Alta to make the final declaration without, finally, the refrain of fear. The poem works to make language (and people) honest. It works to evoke "recognition"—in this way, to heal.

"Could a poem be a cup / to pour our joy into?" she writes in a poem whose title itself supplies the answer: "ANYBODY COULD WRITE THIS POEM. ALL YOU HAVE TO SAY IS YES."

Adrienne Rich: "the field of the poem wired with danger"

Adrienne Rich is a feminist poet who has struggled over a period of many years to become one. She is today one of the strongest and clearest advocates of a feminist philosophy that has changed her poetry, changed her life, by bringing about a closer integration of the one with the other. In 1973 she concludes her poem "Re-forming the Crystal" with this description of the poem—the woman's poem, one element of an interrelated web of act and dream.

> Tonight if the battery charges I want to take the car out on sheet-ice; I want to understand my fear both of the machine and of the accidents of nature. My desire for you is not trivial; I can compare it with the greatest of those accidents. But the energy it draws on might lead to racing a cold engine, cracking the frozen spiderweb, parachuting into the field of the poem wired with danger, or to a trip through gorges and canyons, into the cratered night of female memory, where delicately and with intense care the chieftainess inscribes upon the ribs of the volcano the name of the one she has chosen.[14]

Rich's recent poetry conjoins long open prose lines with tense sharp blunt verse units: whatever forms that will, as she says in "Planetarium," 1968, "translate pulsations / into images."[15] She seeks words that do not lie by standing separate from experience but speak truth through connection to the speaker's own energy and blood. Her poetry offers visions of a patriarchal culture that oppresses, destroys, gives birth only to death; of women being reborn into selfhood, power, and hopefully salvation; of things as they are and as they might be. The poetry that she writes today, its language as well as its themes, is the result of a long process of learning to look "nakedly / at the light" (as she says in "From the Prison House," 1971)[16] and to find the words for what she sees.

Looking back at her early poetry, Rich has written:

> I know that my style was formed first by male poets: by the men I was reading as an undergraduate—Frost, Dylan Thomas, Donne, Auden, MacNiece, Stevens, Yeats. What I chiefly learned from them was craft. But poems are like dreams: in them you put what you don't know you know. Looking back at poems I wrote before I was 21, I'm startled because beneath the conscious craft are glimpses of the split I even then experienced between the girl who wrote poems, who defined herself in writing poems, and the girl who was to define herself by her relationship with men.[17]

W. H. Auden concludes his introduction to her first volume of poems, *A Change of World*, with this praise: "The poems a reader will encounter in this book are neatly and modestly dressed, speak quietly but do not mumble, respect their elders but are not cowed by them, and do not tell fibs; that, for a first volume, is a good deal."[18] Patronizing words, but also truthful; for as a young poet Rich (as well as Auden) accepted the models provided by her patriarchal world and literary tradition. This is poetry with wraps on, carefully, tightly constructed so that the play of words is foregrounded, so that emotion is generalized.

Boundary

What has happened here will do
To bite the living world in two,
Half for me and half for you.
Here at last I fix a line
Severing the world's design
Too small to hold both yours and mine.
There's enormity in a hair
Enough to lead men not to share
Narrow confines of a sphere
But put an ocean or a fence

> Between two opposite intents.
> A hair would span the difference.

Regular meter and rhyme, distance and generalization, combine to create the discrete decorum of her language. This poem refers to profound interpersonal conflict, but who is feeling, what is felt, are never identified, alluded to only as "what has happened here." The nature of the struggle becomes "two opposite intents." While the first six lines refer specifically if obliquely to a "me" and a "you," the issue that the poem is considering, the importance of seemingly small differences, has been generalized by the last six lines: "Enough to lead men not to share." The precision and elegance of the poem with its strongly conceptual vocabulary (of "world," "line," "design," "enormity," "confines," "intents," "difference") helps create the strong but subtle distinctions and boundaries that are described: "Here at last I fix a line / Severing the world's design." Although the poet considers her subject from on high, at all times distant, distinct, objective, that subject is, nevertheless, relationship: specifically, the intimate relationship between woman and man, Rich's abiding concern throughout her career. If into the early work she has put "what you don't know you know," the process of her development as a poet has been to come to consciousness—to know what she knows. The forms and the very language of her poetry have aided in that process as much as they have expressed it:

> Perhaps a simple way of putting it would be to say that instead of poems *about* experiences I am getting poems that *are* experiences, that contribute to my knowledge and my emotional life even while they reflect and assimilate it. In my earlier poems I told you, as precisely and eloquently as I knew how, about something; in the more recent poems something is happening, something has happened to me and, if I have been a good parent to the poem, something will happen to you who read it.[19]

By *Snapshots of a Daughter-in-Law,*[20] a crisp and matter-of-fact statement of ordinary detail ("These old tears in the chopping bowl" ["Peeling Onions"]) balances against the old elaboration of figure. Both are turned more and more to the elucidation of the intimate moment itself, as in these lines from "A Marriage in the Sixties":

> Today we stalk
> in the raging desert of our thought

> whose single drop of mercy is
> each knows the other there.
> Two strangers, thrust for life upon a rock,
> may have at last the perfect hour of talk
> that language aches for; still—
> two minds, two messages.

Talking about the title poem in that volume, Rich calls it still "too literary, too dependent on allusion; I hadn't found the courage yet to do without authorities, or even to use the pronoun 'I.' "[21] The transfers of figurative language can either move away from the particular (as in "Boundary") or into it; in the late fifties and early sixties, Rich's poems are capable of both movements. In "A Marriage in the Sixties" the moment of felt separateness between husband and wife is seen as a kind of intimacy; the quoted lines describe an internal landscape that is bare and full of pain: the mind is a "desert" that is "raging." The single source of life in this barrenness is the fact that each is aware that the other also inhabits the same separate place. Then the focus narrows; the couple are two strangers, thrust for life upon a single rock. The possibility of union ("the perfect hour of talk / that language aches for") is denied by the poem's bleak images of loneliness—"two minds, two messages." Although concentrating upon the moment, Rich's language, with its vocabulary of "thought," "mercy," "life," "talk," "language," "mind," and "messages," is still constantly conceptualizing. In her poetry as in her life, Rich struggles with that primary separation between physical experience and intellectual interpretation.

"Novella," 1962, is a spare poem of literal detail, of quarrel between man and woman, in which separation is revealed and enforced by the verse sentences themselves: each character is confined to her/his own.

> One gets up, goes out to walk.
> (That is the man.)
> The other goes into the next room
> and washes the dishes, cracking one.
> (That is the woman.)

The poem continues accordingly: "She has no blood left in her heart"; "He has forgotten the key." The man leaves and comes back: "The door closes behind him"; he "hears sobbing on the stairs." Suddenly, in the closing two lines, the focus of the poem expands to include the world of which this house and this couple are one small part: "Outside, separate as minds / the stars too come alight." The poem has expanded, as well, into figurative language that aligns internal and external worlds to comment on the universal condition of separation and pain that this woman and this man embody.

Yet Rich has written in a notebook at about this time:

> Paralyzed by the sense that there exists a mesh of relationships—e.g. between my anger at the children, my sensual life, pacifism, sex, (I mean sex in its broadest significance, not merely sexual desire)—an interconnectedness which, if I could see it, make it valid, would give me back myself, make it possible to function lucidly and passionately. Yet I grope in and out among these dark webs.[22]

The existence of such interconnectedness is sensed only during these years; for the world of people and events as she experiences it, as her poems analyze it, gives back nothing but disconnection, separation, loneliness. The "mesh of relationships" is sensed deep within herself but is refused entry into the world.

It might be that language could be the midwife for such a birth. The first stanza of "The Well" (*Snapshots of a Daughter-in-Law*) lists discrete objects that have fallen into a well ("an old trash barrel") in November: leaves, cores of eaten apples, scraps of paper. The second stanza includes the presence of the poet and her attempt to bring about wholeness with her language, "that word."

> But I come, trying
> to breathe that word
> into the well's ear
> which could make the leaves fly up
> like a green jet
> to clothe the naked tree,
> the whole fruit leap to the bough,
> the scraps like fleets of letters
> sail up into my hands.

In this vision of possibility, figurative language again makes its entrance into the poem. The well is personified (it has an ear) and is thus related to the human world. The leaves would return like birds, like water to clothe a body-tree, so that many elements in nature unite in the act; language itself (the scraps of paper) would become boats, bearing messages into her hands. In other words, the vision of wholeness and connection between seasons and persons and things is achieved in the poem through figures of speech that connect what have hitherto been discrete units of experience. Yet even in this poem, which remains language and not physical act, the wholeness is viewed as possibility only. That is because language itself is suspect.

In "Two Songs," 1964, from *Necessities of Life,*[23] Rich discovers in trying to write about her own experience of sexuality a difficulty in using the language ordinarily assigned to it: "sex, as they harshly call it"; "that old 'last act.'" Each of the two short poems is a movement between an existing vocabulary, which must instruct sensation as much as it describes it ("and longing for that young man / pierced me to the roots / bathing every vein, etc.") and her own unnamed truth of feeling.

> Sex, as they harshly call it,
> I fell into it this morning
> at ten o'clock, a drizzling hour
> of traffic and wet newspapers.
> I thought of him who yesterday
> clearly didn't
> turn me to a hot field
> ready for ploughing,
> and longing for that young man
> piercéd me to the roots
> bathing every vein, etc.

She lodges this experience in her own actuality, enumerating hour and weather. Naming it "sex," she tries to use the literary language for it. Except that he "clearly didn't"—and in her poem that phrase is one line juxtaposed against the language of literary cliché—"turn me to a hot field."

> All day he appears to me
> touchingly desirable,
> a prize one could wreck one's peace for.
> I'd call it love if love
> didn't take so many years
> but lust too is a jewel
> a sweet flower and what

pure happiness to know
all our high-toned questions
breed in a lively animal.

She identifies the man as "desirable" and "a prize"; can't call what she feels "love" because the definition she knows for love won't work here; ends by calling it lust and redefining that term to fit with metaphors that could do as well for love: jewel, sweet flower. The ending of the poem is ambivalent, skirting the language issue and opting for the validity of lust, now that she's named it that, for the animality of thoughtful humans. But the second song centers once more on language.

This poem's beginning parallels the start of the first, offering a cliché definition of sex, "that old 'last act,' " followed immediately in the next line by a demurral, "And yet sometimes." Trying to talk about her feeling of being outside herself ("all seems post coitum triste / and I a mere bystander"), she takes literally and develops dramatically yet another sexual cliché: "Somebody else is going off, / getting shot to the moon." A moon race! The couple lie at a crater edge, she arriving split seconds after he does. Then he speaks:

in a different language
yet one I've picked up
through cultural exchanges . . .
we murmur the first moonwords:
Spasibo. Thanks. O. K.

Now Rich specifically equates that other language, the one that is foreign to her but which she has "picked up" and learned to use, as that of men. In later books, she will focus all of her energies on forging a new language, because the language of a patriarchy is both false and destructive. But here she is still at the point of identifying its essential alienness to her; with wit she is playing with the images that such an observation has offered her.

By 1968, in "Implosions" (*Leaflets*), she can clearly identify her purpose as an artist working with language: "I wanted to choose words that even you / would have changed by"; "Take the word / of my pulse, loving and ordinary."[24] (In 1972 she will say "that people turn to what they at least call poetry when they're trying to break out of an extreme situation. Because poetry's got that incredible connection with speech. It seems like almost the most human thing you can do." When the interviewer asks her when these urgent voices turn into poems, she answers: "When it's the voice of someone who knows the rhythm of her own energy and blood.")[25] In "Implosions" she shows herself as aware of the extremity of her situation—"All wars are useless to the dead"—and of the difficulty of bringing about the peace through change that she desires:

> My hands are knotted in the rope
> and I cannot sound the bell
>
> My hands are frozen to the switch
> and I cannot throw it
>
> The foot is in the wheel

Difficult because she is caught in the very situation that she needs to change, as her images show. The primary situation is still the sexual one, so that the need is somehow to unite with the enemy:

> Send out your signals, hoist
> your dark scribbled flags
> but take
> my hand

The poem makes language the metaphor, the means ("signals," "dark scribbled flags") for connecting. The poet now knows she must do more than describe that loneliness and separation, as she used to do, for its implications are more deadly than she had understood. "But revolutionary force has got to have behind it so much more understanding of what we're all about, of whether a whole new set of relationships is possible. It has to begin at the sexual level."[26] She has to try to help:

> When it's finished and we're lying
> in a stubble of blistered flowers
> eyes gaping, mouths staring
> dusted with crushed arterial blues
>
> I'll have done nothing
> even for you?

The change in Rich's thinking about language and its relation to society must necessarily lead to changes in her own poetry. In her earlier work, she generalized and universalized her concern with the personal to make it acceptable as poetry. Abstractions combined with the extensions of figure helped accomplish this for her. But now she sees the essential rather than arbitrary or superficial connection between private and public. She begins to place thematic focus directly upon "the lovers' bed" but still has the problem of having to make the connections with language. In their very form, many of the poems in *Leaflets* show her struggle:

> Something broken Something
> I need By someone
> I love Next year
> will I remember what
> This anger unreal
>   yet
> has to be gone through
> The sun to set
> on this anger
>   I go on
> head down into it
> The mountain pulsing
> Into the oildrum drops
> the ball of fire.
>
> ("Nightbreak")

Rich is breaking down poetic language itself in order to be able to recompose it.

In *The Will to Change* and *Diving into the Wreck*, a new quality of language irradiates Rich's poetry. Many of the poems themselves are manifestos of her new aesthetic:

> I have been standing all my life in the
> direct path of a battery of signals
> the most accurately transmitted most
> untranslatable language in the universe
> I am a galactic cloud so deep so invo-
> luted that a light wave could take 15
> years to travel through me And has
> taken I am an instrument in the shape
> of a woman trying to translate pulsations

into images   for the relief of the body
and the reconstruction of the mind.
("Planetarium," 1968)

The rhythms of this inner focusing are steadier, longer; pauses occur as breaths within the line as well as after it; statement is permissible—any language form that will translate "pulsations into images," as she now identifies the work that must be done.

Complementary to "Planetarium" is another manifesto, written three years later in 1971, "From the Prison House," describing "another eye" that has opened underneath her lids. This eye "looks nakedly / at the light." It observes the external world and sees "detail not on TV," such as "the fingers of the policewoman / searching the cunt of the young prostitute."

This eye
is not for weeping
its vision
must be unblurred

though tears are on my face

its intent is clarity
it must forget
nothing

Here the form is sharp, short, blunt, literal. This eye looks out, not in, so that the two poems taken together are mirror images of the same process. There is urgency in the looking "From the Prison House," which its staccato lines communicate. "What we see, we see / and seeing is changing," she writes in "The Blue Ghazals" (*The Will to Change*). In order to succeed, the sight must be unblurred, excruciatingly clear. One way to translate seen images into words is to pare language, likewise, to its essence, to reduce words to clear unshadowed counters, bone black on the white page. For "this is the oppressor's language," as she observes in a long poem on the subject, "The Burning of Paper instead of Children" (*The Will to Change*); "Yet I need to talk to you." This talking must be done with scrupulous care, being aware at all times of that language.

Our Whole Life

Our whole life a translation
the permissible fibs

and now a knot of lies
eating at itself to get undone

Words bitten thru words

meanings burnt-off like paint
under the blowtorch

All those dead letters
rendered into the oppressor's language

Trying to tell the doctor where it hurts
like the Algerian
who walked from his village, burning

his whole body a cloud of pain
and there are no words for this

except himself
(1969, from *The Will to Change*)

This poem identifies language as absolutely central to the act of living as well as to the art of poetry; central to the identification of the self, to the relation between selves. Its primary metaphor begins the poem: Life = a translation; it equates language and lives. With a series of such metaphors, the poem urges that the most important action of our lives be to live the truth. The poem's own words become agents of the truth that lies beneath the knot of lies; each new metaphor functions like "the blowtorch" to burn to the meanings underneath. The final image insists upon the truth of metaphor itself. Lives are language, and the words we use to show this must come from the same place as the breath itself: "there are no words for this / except himself."

Thus work on language does not exist in a separate compartment from other political enterprises as Rich understands it in the late sixties and early seventies. To resee and reexpress: see the existing damages and dangers, express the realities that have been hidden or lied about or have not yet been born: this is her purpose as a feminist desirous of saving the culture, and poetry can be one medium in which this action occurs.

> We need a poetry which will dare to explore, and to begin exploding, the phallic delusions which are now endangering consciousness itself.[27]
>
> I don't know how or whether poetry changes anything. But neither do I know how or whether bombing or even community organizing changes anything when we are pitted against a massive patriarchal system armed with supertechnology. I believe in subjectivity—that a lot of male Left leaders have turned into Omnipotent Administrators, because their "masculinity" forced them to deny their subjectivity. I believe in dreams and visions and "the madness of art." And at moments I can conceive of a woman's movement that will show the way to humanizing technology and fusing dreams and skills and visions and reason to begin the healing of the human race.[28]
>
> One thing I am sure of: just as woman is becoming her own midwife, creating herself anew, so man will have to learn to gestate and give birth to his own subjectivity—something he has frequently wanted women to do for him. We can go on trying to talk to each other, we can sometimes help each other, poetry and fiction can show us what the other is going through; but women can no longer be primarily mothers and muses for men: we have our own work cut out for us.[29]

"Subjectivity" becomes a key word in Rich's recent discussion of politics and art, because it is that force that must be recognized, validated, and included in any endeavor if the real interrelation between private and public, inner and outer, is to occur. For herself as poet, subjectivity means finding words and images that can establish those connections. Yet Rich is always a thinking and thoughtful woman; she does not, as T. S. Eliot wrote (albeit questionably) about the English metaphysical poets, "feel [her] thought as immediately as the odour of a rose."[30] She is no Alta—nor need she be! In her recent poetry, she includes the subjective by offering clear, careful depictions of an ordinary world that is always symbolic because its terrain is *both* inner and outer: the world of dream and of waking.

> The tragedy of sex
> lies around us, a woodlot
> the axes are sharpened for.
> The old shelters and huts
> stare through the clearing with a certain resolution
> —the hermit's cabin, the hunters' shack—
> scenes of masturbation

and dirty jokes.
A man's world. But finished.
They themselves have sold it to the machines. . . .

Nothing will save this. I am alone,
kicking the last rotting logs
with their strange smell of life, not death,
wondering what on earth it all might have become.
("Waking in the Dark," from *Diving into the Wreck*)

even you, fellow-creature, sister,
sitting across from me, dark with love,
working like me to pick apart
working with me to remake
this trailing knitted thing, this cloth of darkness,
this woman's garment, trying to save the skein.
("When We Dead Awaken," from *Diving into the Wreck*)

"The tragedy of sex" = "a woodlot / the axes are sharpened for"; "this trailing knitted thing, this cloth of darkness, / this woman's garment" is at the same time a literal piece of knitting and a symbolic form for the lives of women. This is the kind of image that Rich creates out of the pulsations she experiences; with the stark lucidity that has become the primary characteristic of her poetic language, she envisions the world of masculine destructiveness, the world of women attempting rebirth in (and on) their own terms.

More and more she sees beyond the present moment into the process that will create a new world. Everywhere in her poetry a fire of creativity rises up against man's ice of impotence.

raking his body down to the thread
of existence
burning away his lie
leaving him in a new
world; a changed
man
("The Phenomenology of Anger," 1972)

. . . the mirror of the fire
of my mind, burning as if it could go on
burning itself, burning down

feeding on everything
till there is nothing in life
that has not fed that fire
("Burning Oneself Out," 1972)

we talk of destruction and creation
ice fists itself around each twig of the lilac
like a fist of law and order
your imagination burns like a bulb in the frozen soil
the fierce shoots knock
at the roof of waiting

when summer comes the ocean may be closed for good
we will turn
to the desert
where survival
takes naked and fiery forms
("Blood-Sister," 1973)

. . . Dawn is the test, the agony
but we were meant to see it:
After this, we may sleep, my sister,
while the flames rise higher and higher, we can sleep.
("White Night," 1974)

In articulating these images of the mind, bringing them into consciousness and into focus in black words on white paper in the waking world, she is helping to bring about the new world. Her focus is on the process for change, and all of these visions of possibility begin in the carefully observed domestic world. "White Night," the ending of which I have just quoted, begins: "Light at a window. Someone up / at this snail-still hour." An everyday (or everynight) event, yet pulsing with political significance, as the following lines that complete the image indicate: ". . . I've had to guess at her / sewing her skin together as I sew mine / though / with a different / stitch." This form, validating the personal, fusing the private and the public, is feminine and feminist.

The change in Rich's poetry has represented her attempt to "function lucidly and passionately" in the world by bringing her sense of interconnectedness into it by means of the poem. Her early work articulated the separation she saw between people in the world, between herself and the world, between aspects of her self, between her self and the poem. Her poetic language created those separations in art by forms that distanced, generalized, impersonalized experience. Her work on language has been to use it as a force for integration, for permitting the subjective entry into the world. Rich's language, broken down and reformed, is now a living extension of her mind. Her poetic images integrate dream acts and waking acts in a conceptual but physically precise way—what I have earlier called surrealism.

Consequently, when she describes the poem itself in 1974, it is solid, active, ordinary, and full of power; it is a part of the world and an act towards the new one; it contains within itself the fire of birth. These words conclude a poem called "The Fact of a Doorframe":

> Now, again, poetry
> violent, arcane, common,
> hewn of the commonest living substance
> into archway, portal, frame
> I grasp for you, your bloodstained splinters, your
> ancient and stubborn poise
> —as the earth trembles—
> burning out from the grain

Feminist Poetry: "violent, arcane, common"

Adrienne Rich and Alta are very different kinds of poets, even as they are very different kinds of women. Yet each speaks as a woman, and each seeks a language that will honestly express that self. In her own way, each poet has used her art to validate the personal and the private as legitimate topics for public speech; each has used her words to integrate the private and the public. Each has seen poetry to be an aspect of political feminism, and as a poet each has based the revolution in the language act, reshaping words into forms that can give us lives, and life: re-forming the crystal.

There is also an important difference between the poetry of Rich and Alta. Rich has worked hard and well to create a form that will articulate her radical politics, but that form itself is not radical. First, because Rich's new forms are still a development from her old. Her feminism has brought her to a place where poetry and self are not at odds but at one, but that self did learn its craft in the fifties, and that self is primarily controlled by the mind. Rich is an intellectual, and her poetry, which is mind-poetry, works by blowing *our* minds. Her forms are neither shocking nor threatening, although her ideas may be. Alta's poetry, on the other hand, confronts the reader in the pit of her stomach, in the genitals, in places that are not traditionally associated with the high art of poetry. Which is the point. Alta's art is not high but low, not elitist but popular, not timeless but time-bound, not universal but particular. Her feminist aesthetics, hand in hand with her personal inclinations, demand this. Alta's very forms—her vocabulary, her literalness, her brevity (the epigram is inferior to the epic, says tradition)—are radical and shocking and threatening. How does one evaluate such poetry? But is it good?

My own answer to these questions is that a poem works if it lives up to itself; if it fulfills the requirements that it has set up for itself. The philosopher Kenneth Burke defined form as the arousing and fulfilling of desires,[31] a definition that includes the reader in a similar process. Such a definition contains no built-in ranking system: it does not call one form better than another. Yet a poem can work and not be good. It can be dull or ordinary or superficial in its solutions and statements. A good poem works powerfully and accurately to communicate between poet and reader or listener. When the power and accuracy of the words in their created form link poet and poem and reader in an instant of light, that, to me, is a good poem. When Alta achieves the distillation and subsequent expansion that I have described, when her poems are tight as a fist, when every word works not only better than any other word in its place could work but also with excitement and power, then Alta is very good. Yet Alta will print poems that do not work this well simply because of their message, their theme or statement. At this point, I think, politics and art part company. And I can continue to respect the political philosophy that tells Alta to print the lines, even if I do not want to call the lines poetry.

Rich's early poetry usually works, and for many years it has been considered good. But its success seems to be a technical one, and those granting the mantle did not seem to be concerned about the excitement of language that is part of a communication process created only when the poet is connected to her poem. Here my criteria differ from that of some other critics, for while I can appreciate a cold pure form, I do not, anymore, usually like it. Today Rich writes as herself, using all her skill with language to that end and purpose. I think she is very good.

But is it poetry? Not only Rich and Alta, but all women who write as women, each woman who writes as herself, continue to face this ultimate of questions. The question comes from the heart of sexism, from the heart of a culture that has made rules for everything, including art, that uphold its values. Women's poetry is so threatening because it does provoke the ultimate questions. It is not that everything women do as poets is different from what men do, or that women use words in ways that men don't, or can't, but that many of their ways are different, and that their ways are for the purpose of expressing in art their real selves, not the selves that have been created for them. To do this in a patriarchy is revolutionary.

Establishment poets and critics are forever talking about timelessness and transcendence and universality in art, condemning many women and minority artists, in accordance with these criteria, as being "limited," or as nonartists. By not universal they mean, however, not including me, the man. The traditional criteria for poetry have described the poetry that men have made; it has been "universal" because it has described the experience of MANkind.

Webster defines a poem as "an arrangement of words in verse; especially a rhythmical composition, sometimes rhymed, expressing facts, ideas, or emotions in a style more concentrated, imaginative, and powerful than that of ordinary speech." A poet is "a person who writes poems." Poetry is "poems, poetical works, the writing of poetry." These broad definitions do not exclude Alta; it is applied and culture-bound criteria that exclude her. Yet the very concentration, imagination, and, above all, power of feminist poetry today threaten the patriarchy because it *is* poetry, and because, whether or not they acknowledge its right to existence, whether or not they stamp it with the seal of approval, POEM, it goes on working as poetry ought, to affect minds, lives, and culture itself.

NOTES

1. *Diving into the Wreck* (New York: W. W. Norton, 1973), back cover.
2. David Kalstone, "Talking with Adrienne Rich," *The Saturday Review: The Arts* 4, no. 17 (April 22, 1972): 57.

3. "Three Conversations," in Barbara and Albert Gelpi, eds., *Adrienne Rich's Poetry* (New York: W. W. Norton, 1975), p. 114.
4. Mary Mackey, "Women's Poetry: Almost Subversive," *Small Press Review* 11, vol. 3, no. 3: 17.
5. Ibid., p. 17.
6. *I Am Not a Practicing Angel* (Trumansburg, New York: The Crossing Press, 1975), p. 8.
7. Her work has been published in such anthologies as Florence Howe and Ellen Bass, eds., *No More Masks: An Anthology of Poems by Women* (New York: Anchor Books, 1973); Elaine Gill, ed., *Mountain Moving Day: Poems by Women* (Trumansburg, New York: The Crossing Press, 1973); Jean Malley and Halé Tokay, eds., *Contemporaries* (New York: The Viking Press, 1972).
8. *No Visible Means of Support* (San Lorenzo, California: Shameless Hussy Press, 1971), p. 30.
9. *Letters to Women* (San Lorenzo, California: Shameless Hussy Press, n.d.).
10. *I Am Not a Practicing Angel*, pp. 51, 80.
11. Elaine Gill, Introduction to *Mountain Moving Day*, p. 8.
12. "Tell It Like It Is," *Small Press Review* 11, vol. 3, no. 3: 3.
13. *No Visible Means of Support*, p. 41. The remaining poems quoted are from this collection.
14. *Poems: Selected and New, 1950–1974* (New York: W. W. Norton, 1975), p. 228.
15. *The Will to Change* (New York: W. W. Norton, 1971), p. 13.
16. *Diving Into the Wreck*, p. 17.
17. "When We Dead Awaken: Writing as Re-Vision," *College English* 34 (October 1972): 21–22.
18. W. H. Auden, Introduction to *A Change of World* (New Haven: Yale University Press, 1951), p. ii.
19. "Poetry and Experience: Statement at a Poetry Reading, 1964," in Gelpi and Gelpi, eds., *Adrienne Rich's Poetry*, p. 89.
20. *Snapshots of a Daughter-in-Law* (New York: W. W. Norton, 1967).
21. "When We Dead Awaken: Poetry as Re-Vision," p. 24.
22. Ibid.
23. *Necessities of Life* (New York: W. W. Norton, 1966), p. 22.
24. *Leaflets* (New York: W. W. Norton, 1969), p. 42.
25. Kalstone, "Talking with Adrienne Rich," p. 58.
26. Ibid.
27. "Caryatid," *The American Poetry Review* 2, no. 3 (May/June, 1973): 11.
28. Kalstone, "Talking with Adrienne Rich," p. 59.

29. "When We Dead Awaken: Writing as Re-Vision," p. 25.
30. T. S. Eliot, *Selected Essays* (New York: Harcourt, Brace & Co., 1950), p. 247.
31. Kenneth Burke, "Lexicon Rhetoricae" in *Counter-Statement* (Los Altos, California: Hermes, 1953), p. 124.

9

The New Tradition

The new tradition exists: wrought slowly through the century with pain and with daring, it daily encounters and confronts a growing audience. No one style or form defines it, yet certain qualities do characterize the poetry of contemporary women poets: a voice that is open, intimate, particular, involved, engaged, committed. It is a poetry whose poet speaks as a woman, so that the form of her poem is an extension of herself. A poetry that is linked to experience through the active participation of the poet herself. A poetry that seeks to affect actively its audience. A poetry that is real, because the voice that speaks it is as real as the poet can be about herself. A poetry that is revolutionary, because by expressing the vision of real women it challenges the patriarchal premises of society itself. Revolutionary, too, because it does connect poet and poem and reader in an instant of light. Because, both "naked and fiery," it touches, and "touching was and still is and will always / be the true / revolution."[1]

It is essential to realize, as I hope this book has made clear, that contemporary women's poetry did not emerge overnight like a wonderful beanstalk but has its roots in the work of women poets well back into the beginnings of the century. Each tentative or purposeful move has been necessary, for the organic metaphor that I have used seems accurate as well as fitting to discuss this women's tradition.

Each voice has helped the birth along. The breathless matter-of-fact startling voice of Dickinson, her taut words etched upon herself, always expanding the confines of mind and poem. The ironic fastidious sharp-edged voice of Moore, making poem puzzles that dazzle, awe, and tease the reader towards wisdom. The domestic meditative voice of Levertov, sensitive to the deep forces behind her mind, to the "terrible joy" of the quotidian, trying to form words that will reveal the meanings necessary to spiritual understanding. The bright sharp violent voice of Plath, who fiercely struggles for purity and unity, who kidnaps the bleeding world into her mind and poem to freeze it, but who cannot live there herself. The wry chanting worldly voice of Sexton, making words into magic scalpels to open up the insides of those people and acts that hurt, turning psychic pain into bitter rituals. The proud tough eloquent voice of Brooks, whose words build a stage on which her people move with grace and braveness. The fiery funny warm rapping voice of Giovanni, telling poems that swing, shout, croon, reach out to make you want to hug her back, to get up and dance along. The straight strong challenging voice of Alta, who makes words into fists and thumbs her nose at you with them, who makes words into love gifts that she offers, laughing, from her pain and shyness. The urgent passionately lucid voice of Rich, seeking language irradiated with a white heat that will with an unremitting clarity and precision reveal the waking or dreaming visions of the mind and thus reshape the world.

Surely today's poetry is equally linked to those other solitary voices—Emily Brontë, Christina Rossetti, Elizabeth Barrett Browning, in nineteenth-century England, Anne Bradstreet in seventeenth-century America, Anne Finch, Countess of Winchilsea, in sixteenth-century England, back to Sappho in ancient Greece—who have always somehow managed to be heard, but the purpose of this book has been to look at the point in time and space when the solitary voice can sing in a chorus, when the word "tradition" begins to apply.

Now that there is a recognizable tradition, what might it achieve, and what will become of it?

I have already spoken of this achievement. I think that the new feminist poetry can help to break the double bind, to validate women as people and as artists and thus begin to bring about a society in which whole people are a possibility. Women's poetry is already changing the nature of poetry itself: its forms and themes, its styles of presentation, its audience.

But I am frequently asked whether this new tradition might be dangerous, to women as well as men, because it keeps us separate from the mainstream, because it seems to be establishing an alternate place and does not try to integrate itself into the real world. Why not all be people together, rather than women and men? Why not just be poets, androgynous creators for whom sex is no longer a hang-up?

A possible goal, but not possible, to my mind, at the present time. On the contrary, I think that the advocacy of Androgyny Now is dangerous to women and to men. For that "mainstream" or "real world" to which its proponents refer is still the patriarchy, even as the very term "androgyny" has historically meant subsuming the feminine into the masculine psyche.[2] We need to give women and all their expressions of themselves the time and space to change the real word so that it becomes a viable place in which to be. In terms of poetry, there must be time for the poetry of women to truly influence new generations of male poets, even as the poetry of men might come to influence new generations of women poets without attacking or co-opting their sense of identity. When poetry by women is finally legitimate and valid, it will not be separate but a viable part of what is "happening." This will have to be a process, and it seems likely that it will be a slow one. Because the situation in poetry, in the arts, is a reflection of the state of the culture as a whole even as it is a stimulus upon it. Art and life are interdependent, spiraling together towards change. Such a fundamental change as an end to patriarchy, one that has been and will no doubt continue to be so *resisted,* must come slowly if it is to come profoundly. The work now, although more painful than the easier "human liberation," is to make the change occur.

Although the new tradition of modern American poetry by women has been defined by the fact that its poets wrote out of a double bind, the tradition itself has been a major force towards breaking the binds. Women need not be crippled and oppressed to write poetry, making art despite society. When women write poetry out of wholeness rather than fragmentation, out of safety rather than fear, out of gladness rather than anger, out of freedom rather than constriction, out of sanity rather than madness, they will still write as women and not androgynes, and the tradition will have reached full flower. We will then be writing our best poetry, in a world that will be able to recognize it and experience it fully.

NOTES

1. Nikki Giovanni, *My House* (New York: William Morrow, 1972), p. 37.
2. Barbara Charlesworth Gelpi, "An Androgynous Aesthetic," in Karen Borden and Faneil Rinn, eds., *Feminist Literary Criticism: A Symposium* (San Jose, California: Diotima Press, 1974), p. 6.

A Selected Bibliography

Anthologies of Poetry by Women

Bernikow, Louise, ed. *The World Split Open: Four Centuries of Women Poets in England and America, 1552–1950.* New York: Vintage Books, 1974.

Chester, Laura, and Barba, Sharon, eds. *Rising Tides: Twentieth Century American Women Poets.* New York: Washington Square Press, 1973.

Efros, Susan. *This Is Women's Work: An Anthology of Prose and Poetry.* San Francisco: Panjandrum Press, 1974.

Gill, Elaine. *Mountain Moving Day: Poems by Women.* Trumansburg, New York: The Crossing Press, 1973.

Howe, Florence, and Bass, Ellen, eds. *No More Masks: An Anthology of Poems by Women.* New York: Anchor Press, 1973.

Iverson, Lucille, and Ruby, Kathryn, eds. *We Become New: Poems by Contemporary American Women.* New York: Bantam Books, 1975.

James, Nancy E., ed. *I, That Am Every Stranger: Poems on Women's Experience.* New Wilmington, Pennsylvania: Globe Printing Co., 1974.

Konek, Carol, and Walters, Dorothy, eds. *I Hear My Sisters Saying.* New York: Thomas Y. Crowell Company, 1975.

Segnitz, Barbara, and Rainey, Carol, eds. *Psyche: The Feminine Poetic Consciousness. An Anthology of Modern American Women Poets.* New York: Dell Publishing Company, 1973.

Stanford, Ann, ed. *The Women Poets in English: An Anthology*. New York: McGraw-Hill Book Company, 1972.

Emily Dickinson

Johnson, Thomas, ed. *The Letters of Emily Dickinson*. 3 vols. Cambridge, Mass.: Harvard University Press, 1958.
———. *The Complete Poems of Emily Dickinson*. Boston: Little, Brown and Company, 1960.
———. *Final Harvest: Emily Dickinson's Poems*. Boston: Little, Brown and Company, 1961.

Marianne Moore

Predilections. New York: The Viking Press, 1955. (Essays.)
A Marianne Moore Reader. New York: The Viking Press, 1961.
The Complete Poems of Marianne Moore. New York: The Viking Press, 1967.

Denise Levertov

The Double Image. London: The Cresset Press, 1946.
Here and Now. San Francisco: City Lights, 1957.
Overland to the Islands. New York: Jargon Books, 1958.
With Eyes at the Back of Our Heads. New York: New Directions, 1959.
The Jacob's Ladder. New York: New Directions, 1961.
O Taste and See. New York: New Directions, 1964.
The Sorrow Dance. New York: New Directions, 1966.
Relearning the Alphabet. New York: New Directions, 1970.
To Stay Alive. New York: New Directions, 1971.
Footprints. New York: New Directions, 1972.
The Poet in the World. New York: New Directions, 1973. (Essays.)

Sylvia Plath

The Colossus and Other Poems. New York: Vintage Books, 1968.
Ariel. New York: Harper and Row, 1968.
Crossing the Water. New York: Harper and Row, 1971.
Winter Trees. New York: Harper and Row, 1972.
The Bell Jar. New York: Bantam Books, 1972. (Novel.)

Anne Sexton

To Bedlam and Part Way Back. Boston: Houghton Mifflin, 1960.

All My Pretty Ones. Boston: Houghton Mifflin, 1962.
Live or Die. Boston: Houghton Mifflin, 1966.
Love Poems. Boston: Houghton Mifflin, 1969.
Transformations. Boston: Houghton Mifflin, 1971.
The Book of Folly. Boston: Houghton Mifflin, 1972.
The Death Notebooks. Boston: Houghton Mifflin, 1974.
The Awful Rowing Towards God. Boston: Houghton Mifflin, 1975.

Gwendolyn Brooks

Selected Poems. New York: Harper and Row, 1963.
Riot. Detroit: Broadside Press, 1969.
Family Pictures. Detroit: Broadside Press, 1970.
The World of Gwendolyn Brooks. New York: Harper and Row, 1971. (Contains *A Street in Bronzeville*, 1945; *Annie Allen*, 1949; *Maud Martha*, 1953, a novel; *The Bean Eaters*, 1960; and *In the Mecca*, 1968.)
Report from Part One. Detroit: Broadside Press, 1972. (Autobiography.)

Nikki Giovanni

Black Feeling, Black Talk/Black Judgement. New York: William Morrow, 1970.
Re: Creation. Detroit: Broadside Press, 1970.
Gemini: An Extended Autobiographical Statement on My First Twenty-Five Years of Being a Black Poet. New York: The Viking Press, 1971. (Essays.)
My House. New York: William Morrow, 1971.
———, and Baldwin, James. *A Dialogue*. New York: J. B. Lippincott, 1973. (Essay.)
———, and Walker, Margaret. *A Poetic Equation*. Washington, D.C.: Howard University Press, 1974. (Essay.)

Alta

Freedom's in Sight. San Lorenzo, California: Shameless Hussy Press, n.d.
Letters to Women. San Lorenzo, California: Shameless Hussy Press, 1970.
Poems and Prose by Alta. Pittsburgh: KNOW Press, 1970.
Burn This and Memorize Yourself. Washington, N.J.: Times Change Press, 1971.
Song of the Wife / Song of the Mistress. San Lorenzo, California: Shameless Hussy Press, 1972.

No Visible Means of Support. San Lorenzo, California: Shameless Hussy Press, 1972.

True Story. Oakland, California: Mama's Press, 1973.

Momma: A Start on All the Untold Stories. Washington, N.J.: Times Change Press, 1974.

I Am Not a Practicing Angel. Trumansburg, N.Y.: Crossing Press, 1975.

Pauline and the Mysterious Pervert. New York: Gotham, 1975.

Adrienne Rich

A Change of World. New Haven: Yale University Press, 1951.

The Diamond Cutters. New York: Harper and Row, 1955.

Necessities of Life. New York: W. W. Norton, 1966.

Snapshots of a Daughter-in-Law. New York: W. W. Norton, 1967.

Leaflets. New York: W. W. Norton, 1969.

The Will to Change. New York: W. W. Norton, 1971.

Diving into the Wreck. New York: W. W. Norton, 1973.

Poems: Selected and New, 1950–1974. New York: W. W. Norton, 1975.

Gelpi, Barbara Charlesworth, and Gelpi, Albert, eds. *Adrienne Rich's Poetry.* New York: W. W. Norton, 1975. (Contains a selection of poems and essays by the poet, as well as reviews and criticism.)

Additions to bibliography (work by the poets published since the completion of this study)

Giovanni, Nikki. *The Women and the Men.* New York: William Morrow, 1975.

Levertov, Denise. *The Freeing of the Dust.* New York: New Directions, 1975.

Plath, Sylvia. *Letters Home: Correspondence 1950–1963.* ed. Aurelia Schober Plath. New York: Harper and Row, 1975.

Sexton, Anne. *45 Mercy Street.* ed. Linda Gray Sexton. Boston: Houghton Mifflin, 1976.